NAZI NEXUS

Also by Edwin Black

www.edwinblack.com

THE PLAN
How to Rescue Society the Day the Oil Stops—or the Day Before
www.planforoilcrisis.com
2008

INTERNAL COMBUSTION
How Corporations and Governments Addicted the World to Oil
and Derailed the Alternatives
www.internalcombustionbook.com
2006

BANKING ON BAGHDAD
Inside Iraq's 7,000 Year History of War, Profit, and Conflict
www.bankingonbaghdad.com
2004

WAR AGAINST THE WEAK
Eugenics and America's Campaign to Create a Master Race
www.waragainsttheweak.com
2003

IBM AND THE HOLOCAUST
The Strategic Alliance Between Nazi Germany
and America's Most Powerful Corporation
www.ibmandtheholocaust.com
2001

THE TRANSFER AGREEMENT
The Dramatic Story of the Pact Between the Third Reich
and Jewish Palestine
www.transferagreement.com
1984 and 2001

FORMAT C: *A Novel*
www.formatnovel.com
1999

To Bill Benjami: Please connect the dots.
9-22-11
150

NAZI NEXUS

America's Corporate Connections to Hitler's Holocaust

BY

EDWIN BLACK

DIALOG PRESS

WASHINGTON, D.C.

To all the corporations
that refuse to create future victims

This book is printed on acid-free paper.

ISBN 978-091415309-2

Printed in the United States of America

13 12 11 10 09   5 4 3 2 1

Cover designed by Tallgrass Studios and Karl Kaufmann

Any changes, corrections, or additions to this book can be found at http://www.nazinexus.com

Contents

Introduction .vii

CHAPTER 1 2
Ford, Jew Hatred, and Political Racism

CHAPTER 2 17
Carnegie, Eugenics, and the Master Race

CHAPTER 3 51
Rockefeller, Mengele, and Eugenics

CHAPTER 4 95
GM and the Motorization of the Reich

CHAPTER 5 127
IBM Organizes the Holocaust

Behind the Nexus

Writing *Nazi Nexus* was inspired by two unexpected events. For years, I had been lecturing at universities, museums, churches, and synagogues on my various books and investigative articles. These include *IBM and the Holocaust, War Against the Weak, The Transfer Agreement, Banking on Baghdad, Internal Combustion*, and such syndicated investigations as "Hitler's Carmaker." I had always spoken on just one of those books at a time.

That changed in November, 2006, when I was invited to deliver two back-to-back Kristallnacht presentations. Neither venue wanted me to speak on just one of my books. They each wanted me to tie together all my major research about American corporate complicity in the Holocaust—from the Ford Motor Company to Carnegie to Rockefeller to General Motors and, of course, IBM. Each of these corporations had a direct involvement in the actual genocide perpetrated by Hitler against the Jews. I found myself speaking and answering questions for hours.

I decided then to connect all the dots of my prior research and portray the scope of the Nazi Nexus. I started with a chapter for a German-language anthology entitled *Das Heilige Nichts (Nothing Sacred)*; other contributors included Pope Benedict XVI. That gave me the determination to synthesize into a single compact book the cold-hearted complicity of some of America's most iconic corporate entities. I limited myself to those firms knowingly engaged in major support for the Holocaust itself, omitting many firms merely engaged in trading with the enemy. Hence, I did not include other guilty parties such as Coke which invented Fanta to enliven Nazi soldiers, Standard Oil which contributed mightily to the Luftwaffe, Eastman Kodak, or hundreds of others which regularly traded with the Reich during the War.

This volume will shock, sadden, and shake many as they look at the monetized evil constructed by the intersection of American corporate force and German genocidal desire. But *Nazi Nexus* should not emerge as a standalone revelation as much as a frightful invitation to further investigate the thick volumes upon whose shoulders *Nazi Nexus* stands. Behind each chapter is a copiously documented book or investigation. This book is not for spot checking. If you cannot read this entire book, do not read it at all. The monster must be viewed completely to be comprehended.

Nazi Nexus is a compilation of prior scholarship. Several dozen pages of acknowledgements can be found in each of my original volumes, listing the scores of research assistants, historians, archivists, and eye witnesses who have shared their labors and their hearts to help bring this information to life. Their names are forever enshrined in the original books. The sources for *Nazi Nexus* are primarily drawn from my other voluminously footnoted, published works. They are preserved in those editions in exhaustive detail.

However, some thanks are in order. First, I would like to thank the United States Holocaust Memorial Museum for refusing to include any of this information in its various exhibits. There is an unwritten taboo at the USHMM about exploring the complicity of American corporations and the Holocaust. This has made my work all the more energized and appreciated by those who want the unvarnished truth.

I would also like to thank the many well-paid Holocaust historians for hire who have been sponsored by implicated corporations to dress up, obscure, spin and/or divert attention away from the towering culpability of these companies. The shame of these firms needs to be illuminated by independent investigation without the filter of bought-and-paid for corporate history. If anything, *Nazi Nexus* is a cry to independent investigative journalists and historians everywhere to independently document this final frontier of Holocaust accountability. The centers of such inquiries must not only be Detroit, New York, or Berlin, but also many centers of corporately endowed academia. After all, Hitler's war against humanity was always wrapped in pseudo-academics, falsely medicalized, coated with fallacious race science and twisted intellectualism.

Ironically, most of these corporations have admitted their crimes and apologized. This includes Ford, Carnegie, Rockefeller and even General Motors. Only IBM has remained silent a decade after the revelations of its genocidal conduct first became known.

Now is a good time to remind the world that the Holocaust would have always occurred with or without assistance from America. But the assistance the Hitler regime did receive enormously magnified the astronomical dimensions and statistics of that genocide. Equally important, we must never deflect blame for the true perpetrators of the Holocaust: Hitler, the Nazis and Nazi supporters and henchmen throughout Germany and in many lands.

Hitler did it. But Hitler had help. *Nazi Nexus* chronicles the type of indispensable help Hitler did receive.

It would be wrong not to mention the events of late 2008 swirling in the background as *Nazi Nexus* finalized. During those months, America and the world witnessed American big business melting down after years of deception, avarice, and lack of accountability. Companies that will go to any lengths to further their misconduct at home find the pathway to misconduct in foreign lands a very short footbridge. Some of the modern day culprits are the same villains that collaborated with Germany during the Reich years. Above all, *Nazi Nexus* is a call to arms for young executives, emerging entrepreneurs, and reflective captains of industry to never again allow their corporate muscle, their technology, and their sheer business prowess to afflict innocent civilians.

Edwin Black
Washington, D.C.
January 1, 2009

CHAPTER ONE

Ford, Jew Hatred, and Political Racism

Persecution of Jews and Jew-hatred have been the bane of Jewish existence for centuries.

Since their expulsion from Judea by the Romans in the first century A.D., Jews have wandered the world in disconsolate if hopeful dislocation and relocation. Denied land or even equal social standing in most of the regions they settled, Jews adopted the only lifestyles available to them—the portable professions. Finance and moneylending, buying and selling itinerantly or in shops, the arts and trades, transport, matters of intellect, and middlemanship of all things. These were the roles Jews were allowed to assume. These were the roles Jews did assume, and ones in which they generally achieved success.

Although the Jewish niche was small compared to the larger society, as outsiders they were often the first to be blamed by local populations when well water went bad, when plague arrived, when economies collapsed and, really, when anything adverse occurred. Germany was no exception; anti-Semitism had become part of the social grain as far back as the Reformation when in 1543, the leader of the Protestant movement, Martin Luther, published *On the Jews and Their Lies.*

Because Jews refused to convert, Luther exhorted the volatile population to fear and destroy their Jewish neighbors. Luther's solution: "First to set fire to their synagogues or schools... Second, I advise that their houses also be razed and destroyed. For they pursue in them the same aims as in their synagogues. Instead they might be lodged under a roof or in a barn, like the gypsies. This will bring home to them that they are not masters in our country as they boast, but that they are living in exile and in captivity, as they incessantly wail and lament about us before God. Third, I advise that all their prayer books and Talmudic writings, in which such idolatry, lies, cursing, and blasphemy are taught, be taken from them." Luther went to demand, "Fourth, I advise that their rabbis be forbidden to teach henceforth on pain of loss of life and limb. ...Fifth, I advise that safe-conduct on the highways be abolished completely for the Jews. For they have no business in the countryside, since they are not lords, officials, tradesmen, or the like. Let them stay at home. Sixth, I advise that usury be prohibited to them, and that all cash and treasure of silver and gold be taken from them and put aside for safekeeping. The reason for such a measure is that, as said above, they have no other means of earning a livelihood than usury, and by it they have stolen and robbed from us all they possess."

For centuries, Luther's solution was resurrected and implemented in part or in whole by various towns and kingdoms when it was useful for the authorities or the local populace to do so. Whether through an unsourced tradition or direct acknowledgement, the Luther program of persecution underlay the bleakest parts of European Jewish history.

But Adolf Hitler took the theme of local Jew-hatred to a dramatic and odious new low. Luther's solution was advocated by Hitler, not only chapter and verse, but with a new political imperative and rationale. No longer was it just a matter of medieval prejudice against an out-group—the Jews. Hitler inculcated a new intellectual anti-Jewish justification for the new intellectual century, and branded the Jew "an international menace" that had to be defeated and destroyed.

According to Hitler, Jews nefariously controlled and manipulated the media, the money, the militaries, and all the mischief in the world. The hidden Jewish goal, he insisted, was the domination of all mankind through conspiratorial organizations. "International Jewry" was a political demon that had to be actively opposed by all Germans as a rational act of defense, Hitler argued. *Der Führer* thus elevated anti-Semitism from a recurring local reaction to a global crusade, from an episodic backlash to a lasting political ideology. This ideology demanded Jewish purges and expulsion from every sector of society—and then communal and literal destruction. Modern anti-Semitism was no longer a manifestation of out-group fear, but the basis for a war for survival.

Where did Hitler discover his radical views on the so-called international Jewish menace? Answer: Henry Ford.

The richest man in America, whose name was stamped on every Model T, quickly catapulted to the forefront of global political anti-Semitism after he became convinced of the Jewish conspiracy cliché. Henry Ford's nineteenth-century rural mentality didn't adapt well to the complexities of the twentieth-century world. He did things in his own peculiar way—regardless of the cost. Ford was a clever if stubborn machine apprentice, production designer, and later a visionary businessman who had successfully cloned earlier hand-built European versions of the internal combustion machine and claimed them as his own inventions. To manufacture them cheaply, Ford literally invented mass production of motor vehicles. Abandoning the notion of hand-crafted excellence, Ford brought the Industrial Revolution's assembly line to the "one-at-a-time" world of the automobile. Indeed, in his day, mass production of cars was known as "Fordism." He singlehandedly revolutionized the field.

Whereas, Ford was a brilliant businessman who excelled in a vast array of commercial efforts, he was intellectually "gullible." Fundamentally, he was uneducated. Ford never graduated from high school. Not a few branded Ford an idiot. Sugar frightened him because he was convinced the sharp edges of the crystals would tear up the stomach, and when his chemist showed him how easily it dissolved, an angry Ford refused to speak to him for weeks.

During a libel deposition, Ford was asked if he knew about the American Revolution. Ford: "I understand there was one in 1812." When pressed for any other dates, he replied, "I don't know of any others." Ever heard of Benedict Arnold? Ford: "Heard the name… I have just forgotten just who he is. He is a writer, I think." Read any good books? Ford: "I don't like to read books, they muss up my mind."

Yet Ford, the populist and new-age hero, was one of the most esteemed and powerful men in America.

Shortly after the Great War began in Europe, Ford claimed he had discovered "proof" that Jews were behind the world's troubles. No one is really sure where Ford obtained the basis for his fraudulent allegations or his determination to lead a crusade against the Jews. Certainly, for years during litigious battles against other automakers and investors, he struggled against Wall Street and bankers both of Jewish descent and of the non-Jewish, J.P. Morgan variety. But through it all, Ford showed friendship to Jewish people—both the Jewish Eastern European immigrant factory workers who he treated with equality and his Jewish friends such as his next door neighbor, Rabbi Leo M. Franklin, who received a free custom-built automobile each year as a birthday present.

The first glimmer of the anti-Jewish Ford might have been early in April 1915 during an interview with *New York Times Magazine*. Reflecting on the mass killing underway in Europe during the Great War, Ford quipped, "Moneylenders and munitions makers cause wars… The warmongers urging military preparedness in America are Wall Street bankers." Moneylenders, munitions makers, and Wall Street bankers were all Ford euphemisms for "the Jews."

A few months later in 1915, Ford summoned reporters to a press conference where he denounced "the parasite known as the absentee owner" as the culprit who "fosters war." He added, "New York wants war, but the United States doesn't." Jotting in his personal notebook, Ford scribbled, replete with misspellings and fragments, "people who profit from war must go… War is created by people who have no country or homes Hadies Hell and live in every other country." All these public outbursts and private remarks were allusions to the Jewish stereotype.

During a morning gathering in his office on November 11, 1915, Ford stunned his guests by breaking free from hazy innuendoes. When the topic of the Great War arose, Ford, as though mesmerized, blurted uncontrollably, "I know who caused the war. The German-Jewish bankers. I have the evidence here. Facts. The German-Jewish bankers caused the war."

Ford began devoting much of his energy, wealth, and prestige to spreading a venomous "revelation" that the Jews were behind all the evils in the world. Within a year, unable to convince the establishment, he set about starting his own newspaper and printing house that he could command at will. He acquired the financially unviable *Dearborn Independent*, placing it under the control of a new company called The Dearborn Publishing Company to be located on Ford Motor Company property in a building near the tractor plant. Ford temporarily left the presidency of the automobile company to become president of the printing company. His wife was appointed vice-president. His son, Edsel, was secretary-treasurer.

Ford dove into the project. He dominated many of the *Dearborn Independent's* editorial meetings, often scrutinized and approved the lead-hued linear lines of type, and even hand-polished the brass knobs on the printing press until they glistened.

On January 11, 1919, the first issue rolled off Ford's vintage nineteenth century presses. The grey-ghost main feature of the broadsheet was "Mr. Ford's Own Page," an assemblage of strident observations about what was wrong with the world. For about a year, the drab *Dearborn Independent* would plod along as a paper and ink extension of Ford's time-warped "plain folks" persona. Ford and his newspaper extolled the virtues of rural life and religion, true grit and good tractors, hunting and horses. At the same time, the paper denounced Wall Street and Wilson, the "Babylons of Jazz" and the Bolsheviks of Moscow, actresses who showed their undergarments, and of course the dark agents of hidden enemies conspiring against the world. The weekly was just plain boring to a War-demobilized, suffragette-ascending, proto-

Roaring Twenties bathtub ginning society—but at five cents per copy via a "please take one" distribution, thousands read and then tossed it.

Everything changed when Ford received a copy of the notorious anti-Jewish hate tale, *the Protocols of the Learned Elders of Zion*.

The incredible *Protocols* told of a sinister—and imaginary— Zionist conclave, during which a cabal of powerful Jews planned to overtake all mankind by manipulating all media, governments, and economies. Through a combination of Capitalism, Communism, stage-managed revolution, and secretly fomented warfare among nations, the Jew would emerge as the victor. The Jewish conspiracy was the hidden force that chewed and tore at the world. These ideas were stolen in part from an 1864 French precursor satire, penned by Maurice Joly and directed not against the Jews but against Napoleon. Titled *Dialogues in Hell between Machiavelli and Montesquieu*, Joly's fantasy-infused diatribe included a misty Prague cemetery scene, complete with satanic rituals, chats with ghosts, and references to Jewish powers.

Decades later, Czarist agents recast sections of Joly's satire as a genuine document, added contemporary references, and forged the fundamentals of the modern *Protocols*. From the end of the nineteenth century, these fake *Protocols* began circulating in Europe, principally Russia, in various forms; sometimes as an underground typescript, sometimes a pamphlet, and from time to time, an excerpted article series. During the so-called Red Scare of 1919, which followed the Bolshevik revolution in Russia, an English translation of *Protocols* made its way into several British and American publications cast mainly as a Bolshevik manifesto. Virtually every time the forged *Protocols* appeared, authoritative figures and journalistic inquiries proved it to be a fantastic, rambling group libel without any merit or factual basis.

Most laughed off the scurrilous *Protocols*. Ford did not. When a copy made its way to him in 1920, he grappled it to his heart as gospel. A misguided and misinformed Ford took it upon himself to spread its gospel to a world wracked by post-War economic and political chaos. Now the *Dearborn Independent* would be Ford's clarion to the world, a call to arms against the Jewish menace, an intrepid voice against an entire race of masterminds clandestinely steering the most sinister plot in history.

In May 1920 it began. A series of *Dearborn Independent* articles and editorials launched, publicizing *the Protocols* and a host of other anti-Semitic slanders and accusations under the general heading, "The International Jew—The World's Problem." Ford's series described a vast Jewish conspiracy to subvert and subjugate America and the world. Ford accused American Jewish leaders such as Louis Marshall and Louis Brandeis of using Presidents Taft and Wilson as their puppets. Other prominent Jews were accused of perpetrating World War I for the benefit of "Jewish Bankers" and fomenting the 1905 Russian Revolution for racial imperialism. The defamations continued for 91 provocative weeks, as Ford's paper denounced the Jewish conspiracy for corruption on Wall Street, in labor, in big media, in cotton and in tobacco. Jews were also allegedly responsible for Benedict Arnold, the Civil War, and even the assassination of Abraham Lincoln. What Jews could not achieve by money, media, or manipulation, they would achieve by pandering to the sexual perversions of the powerful and prominent.

Everything was the fault of the Jews, according to Ford's pronouncements and publications. On baseball: "If fans wish to know the trouble with American baseball, they have it in three words: too much Jew." On post-War problems: "Jews caused the War, the Jews caused the outbreak of thieving and robbery all across the country, the Jews caused the inefficiency of the Navy." On housing problems: "Jews are the largest and most numerous landlords." On jazz: It was just "Jewish moron music." On a perceived flavor change in his favorite candy: "The Jews have taken hold of it."

Ford's accusations were not just the rambling libels of *The Dearborn Independent.* They were in fact a product of the Ford Motor Company. Henry Ford listed his name at the top of every front page. Ford dealers were compelled to buy and sell subscriptions as part of their commercial commitment. Dealers who filled their subscription quotas received Ford cars as prizes. Those falling short were assured that *The Dearborn Independent* was "just as much of a Ford product as the car or tractor." Many reluctant dealers received threatening legalistic letters from the corporation insisting they sell the tabloid. Reprints were bound into booklets and distributed to libraries and YMCAs through the nation. Ultimately, using the techniques of mass production, Ford was able to escalate the *Protocols* from a negligible and disorganized irritant of random circulation to a national sensation of 500,000 copies.

Devoting the national sales force and the assets of Ford Motor Company to spreading Jew hatred made Henry Ford the first to organize anti-Semitism in America. Indeed, he was the hero of anti-Semites the world over. His newspaper series was published as a book, *The International Jew,* translated into many languages, and widely disseminated as authentic fact. Although the work was just a compilation of the hodgepodge *Protocols,* it was proliferated as the work of Henry Ford himself and prominently featured his byline.

After worldwide travels, Jewish activist attorney Samuel Untermeyer complained, "Wherever there was a Ford car, there was a Ford agency not far away, and wherever there was a Ford agency, these vile libelous books in the language of the country were to be found. They, coupled with the magic name of Ford, have done more than could be undone in a century to sow, spread, and ripen the poisonous seeds of anti-Semitism and race hatred."

The marquee name of "Henry Ford" was revered worldwide. He was a larger-than-life figure, hailed a hero for the Tin Lizzie inventiveness that made cars available to the average man; his dramatic advances in employment conditions, including the celebrated $5 per day "living wage" for long-neglected factory workers; his reputation for standing up to the fat cats; and his stubborn independence. From 1916 to 1923, Ford was a constant and prominent mention as a candidate for president. In 1916, he won the Nebraska primary without even campaigning. In 1923, two polls showed him as a distinct front-runner against the biggest party politicians. In the minds of many, the fact that the anti-Semitic accusations bore the gold-plated name "Henry Ford" legitimized—even exalted—the anti-Jewish precepts.

In Germany, where Ford was venerated, *The International Jew* was translated and published in February 1921. It enjoyed six editions in two years with thousands of copies in print. Ford's book quickly became the bible of German anti-Semites and early incarnations of the Nazi party.

Munich Nazis sent Ford's book throughout the country "by the carload," according to the Berlin correspondent of the *Chicago Tribune*. Ford Motor Company in America acknowledged the adoption by producing and shipping thousands of swastika pins to early organizing Nazis in Germany for their own distribution. He met leading Nazi agents in his Detroit office as a sign of solidarity.

Baldur von Schirach was typical of key Germans who were rapt by *The International Jew*. As the doctrinaire head of the Hitler Youth and later the infamous anti-Jewish governor of Nazi-occupied Vienna, he testified at the Nuremburg Trials that long before he joined Hitler's movement, Ford's publication had created his personal anti-Jewish turning point: "The decisive anti-Semitic book which I read at that time," admitted von Schirach, "and the book which influenced my comrades was Henry Ford's book, *The International Jew*. I read it and became anti-Semitic. This book made in those days a great impression on my friends and myself, because we saw in Henry Ford the representative of success, also the representative of a progressive social policy. In the poverty-stricken and wretched Germany of the time, youth looked toward America, and ... it was Henry Ford who, to us, represented America... If he said the Jews were to blame, naturally we believed him."

It was the same for Adolf Hitler himself. *Der Führer* was massively influenced by Ford's book. He read the work at least two years before *Mein Kampf* was written. It shows. In *Mein Kampf*, chapter 11, Hitler wrote, "To what extent the whole existence of this people is based on a continuous lie is shown incomparably by *the Protocols of the Elders of Zion*, so infinitely hated by the Jews. They are based on a forgery, the *Frankfurter Zeitung* moans and screams once every week: [that is] the best proof that they are authentic. ...The important thing is that with positively terrifying certainty they reveal the nature and activity of the Jewish people and expose their inner contexts as well as their ultimate final aims."

Other passages in *Mein Kampf* showed Hitler's fascination with American racial eugenics and either emulated or invoked the concepts he had read in Ford's publications.

Hitler was so entranced with Ford's struggle against Jewish economic power that he hung a large portrait of Ford beside his desk and spoke of him incessantly.

When Hitler was interviewed by a *Chicago Tribune* reporter in 1923 about Ford's chances of winning the U.S. presidency, the Nazi leader enthusiastically declared, "I wish that I could send some of my shock troops to Chicago and other big American cities to help in the elections. We look on Heinrich Ford as the leader of the growing Fascist Party in America." Hitler praised *The International Jew* to the *Chicago Tribune* bragging, "The book is being circulated to millions throughout Germany."

Just before Christmas 1931, *der Führer* admitted to a *Detroit News* reporter, "I regard Henry Ford as my inspiration." Once the Third Reich came to power, millions of Ford's books were circulated to every school and party office in the Germany, many featuring the names Hitler and Ford emblazoned on the cover side-by-side. Ford's work helped warp German minds in every corner of the Reich.

American Jewish reaction to the Henry Ford threat was swift. Within a few months of *The Dearborn Independent's* inaugural anti-Semitic issue in 1920, a spontaneous Jewish boycott movement against Ford erupted. Libel suits were launched against Ford personally. A Jewish-led campaign to legally ban the sale or distribution of the publication began in Chicago, Boston, St. Louis, and other cities. Where legislated bans were overturned by court action, angry mobs often greeted *Dearborn Independent* street vendors.

The backlash campaign started hurting Ford by late 1920, within months of initial publication. Jews *en masse* began refusing to purchase any vehicle bearing a Ford emblem. Typical was a Connecticut Jewish community's 400-car parade in early 1921 honoring Albert Einstein and Zionist leader Chaim Weizmann. Parade rules included the proviso "Positively no Ford machines permitted in line." This movement eventually reached Ford's backyard when his annual birthday gift of a new automobile to neighbor Rabbi Franklin arrived. After the *Dearborn Independent's* articles began, the rabbi emphatically refused Ford's gift.

Even the staunchly conservative American Jewish Committee encouraged the anti-Ford boycott. The Committee opposed proclaiming an "official" boycott, reluctant to openly answer Ford's charges of an economic conspiracy with a coordinated economic weapon. But Committee leader Louis Marshall felt a "silent boycott" would be equally effective, maintaining that any self-respecting Jew would know what to do without being told when purchasing an automobile.

In reality, the Jewish boycott of Ford products was probably not statistically effective. While Ford's sales in urban centers did decrease significantly, equally important sales in small towns and rural areas either remained constant or increased. In truth, the recorded urban sales slumps were only partially due to the Jewish-led boycott. A sharp economic downturn coupled with the declining popularity of the Model T were equally potent factors. But in the early and mid-1920s, Ford people were convinced that the Jewish-led boycott was in large part responsible for their troubles. But boycotts are not measured in dollars and cents as much as by ergs of fear. The very idea bit into the Ford network.

The precise figures were guarded by Ford's corporate sales hierarchy even as dealers and regional sales managers continually pleaded for Ford's campaign to cease. For example, New York sales manager Gaston Plaintiff, a personal friend of Ford, wrote numerous letters bemoaning the boycott. Ford would stubbornly reply, "If they want our product, they'll buy it."

In 1927, the advent of a competitive Chevrolet made the Jewish boycott an unacceptable liability for Ford Motor Company. Any lost product loyalty would now be lost forever to the competition, Ford officials believed. The black and bleak Model T was obsolete. Everyone knew that. The company's future was precariously stacked on a snazzy new Model A, available in colors and featuring enormous technical improvements. At the same time, Ford desperately sought to avoid humiliating public trials with libeled Jews who had sued.

In the summer of 1927, Ford's representatives approached Nathan Perlman, a vice-president of the American Jewish Congress, seeking a truce. Congress president Stephen Wise was in Europe, so Perlman referred Ford's people to the committee. Louis Marshall prepared an embarrassing *retraction cum apology* for Ford to sign and publish. Close advisers cautioned the carmaker that the humiliating apology might be too much for Ford's pride. But the global leader of anti-Semites had endured boycotts, legal actions, and political abrasions long enough.

It was time to make money, secure the future, stop fighting the Jews, and take up arms against Chevrolet.

On July 7, 1927, in the last year of the outmoded Model T—as Ford acknowledged a decline of about a half million fewer cars sold, and as he prepared for a major financial effort to introduce his new Model A—the proud gladiator of anti-Semites released to the press his contrite plea for forgiveness for wronging the Jews and misleading all mankind.

"I have given consideration," wrote Ford, "to the series of articles concerning Jews which have since 1920 appeared in the *Dearborn Independent*... and in pamphlet form under the title *The International Jew*. ...To my great regret, I have learned that Jews generally, and particularly those of this country, not only resent these publications as promoting anti-Semitism, but regard me as their enemy... I am deeply mortified. ...I deem it to be my duty as an honorable man to make amends for the wrong done to the Jews as fellowmen and brothers, by asking their forgiveness for the harm that I have unintentionally committed, by retracting, so far as lies within my power, the offensive charges laid at their door by these publications, and by giving them the unqualified assurance that henceforth they may look to me for friendship and goodwill."

Within weeks the retraction appeared in *The Dearborn Independent* itself. Shortly thereafter, Ford's advertising agencies were instructed to spend about 12 percent of the Model A's $1.3 million introductory advertising in Yiddish and Anglo-Jewish newspapers—the only minority press included in the campaign. Ford also directed that five truckloads of *The International Jew* be burned, and ordered overseas publishers to cease publication.

Ford's capitulation was hit the hardest in Germany among Nazi circles. Nazi anti-Jewish boycott leader Theodor Fritsch wrote to Ford lamenting the loss of both book sales and "the inestimable mental goods" Ford had bestowed upon civilization. "The publication of this book remains the most important action of your life," he stated. Yet now, as Fritsch put it, Ford was capitulating to the financial might of the Jews.

Adolf Hitler, when informed of the retraction, tried to avoid comment. Henry Ford was the man who the Nazi party and *der Führer* himself lionized as the quintessential fighter of the so-called Jewish economic conspiracy. Hitler had once told reporters in Germany that "the struggle of international Jewish finance against Ford... has only strengthened (Nazi) sympathies... for Ford." In an early edition of *Mein Kampf*, Hitler had declared that "only a single great man, Ford," was able to stand up to Jewish economic power.

Ford's unexpected surrender was so powerful a loss to Hitler's movement that the Nazis preferred to ignore the retraction as a mere expediency. Fritsch continued printing *The International Jew*. Nonetheless, the tribute to Ford in *Mein Kampf* was changed in its second edition. The words "only a single great man, Ford," were replaced with the phrase "only a very few" could stand up to Jewish economic power.

Despite the public retraction, Ford's feelings did not change. The Ford Motor Company went on to collaborate with the Third Reich in its efforts to destroy the Jews and conquer neighboring countries, setting up factories to produce vehicles in large part for the SS and the military in preparation for the invasion of Europe. In 1938, in a festive Berlin ceremony, Hitler bestowed upon Ford his special medal of honor, the Grand Cross of the Order of the German Eagle, for "foreigners who have been of special service to the Reich." When awarded, the great sash festooned with swastikas wrapped across Ford's chest from shoulder to hip. The award sparked an outcry from the Jewish community, which demanded he repudiate the medal. Ford simply said to an associate, "They told me to return it or else I'm not American. I'm going to keep it."

After World War II broke out, Ford Motor Company in Detroit helped the Nazis by ordering parts made in Ford's Cologne plant for use in Ford's factories in Latin America and Japan. Even after the U.S. entered the war, and the Reich by necessity placed American companies in receivership as enemy property, the Ford-Nazi relationship was one of global cooperation, awaiting the outcome of the hostilities when Detroit would be able to collect on massive wartime profits. During the war years, Ford's pre-war management was kept in place. Only the profits were temporarily frozen in secure accounts. Ultimately, about a third of the Reich's trucks were manufactured by Ford. A 1945 U.S. Army report called Ford "the arsenal of Nazism" with the "consent" of the company in Dearborn.

With these trucks, Hitler was able to roll across the invaded countries and scoop up victims. It was self-sustaining. Innocent civilians, mainly young people, were kidnapped, transported back to Germany and forced to work in the Ford plant in Cologne. Conditions were brutal, approximating that of some concentration camps. Elsa Iwanowa was one of hundreds of young women kidnapped from her Russian village in 1942 to labor at Ford's Cologne factory. "The conditions were terrible," she recalled in a post-war comment published in the *Washington Post.* "They put us in barracks, on three-tier bunks," adding, "It was very cold; they did not pay us at all and scarcely fed us. The only reason that we survived was that we were young and fit."

Through it all, from the first combative moments in which Hitler discovered unshakeable proof of the Jewish conspiracy to the smoke-filled years when Ford allied with the Reich against all humanity, a lesson had been learned by the Nazis. Jewish boycotts and economic influence, in the Nazi view, held the power not only to subvert governments, but to silence the most indomitable challengers—even Ford himself. It would take something extraordinary to defeat this global pest. What could that be?

Henry Ford's *International Jew*, volume 4, suggested the method in a quoted letter. "Imagine for a moment that there were no Semites in Europe. Would the tragedy be so terrible now? Hardly! …Some day they will reap what they have sown."

Sources: Primary documentation for this chapter is mainly taken from *The Transfer Agreement* by Edwin Black. Additional sources: *American Axis* by Max Wallace, *Henry Ford and the Jews* by Neil Baldwin, and *Henry Ford and the Jews* by Albert Lee.

CHAPTER TWO

Carnegie, Eugenics, and the Master Race

Genetics was the key to how Jews lived and how they died in the Third Reich.

Long before Adolf Hitler ascended to the German chancellorship on January 30, 1933, he concluded that the Jewish enemy he reviled was not merely those that practiced the Jewish religion. His world was more threatened by an invisible menace—those with "Jewish blood," who did not appear to be Jewish. Hitler feared these hidden Jews most. Nazi racial experts called them "carriers."

Under Nazi precepts, Jews handed down their parasitical, virtually bacterial nature from generation to generation as a matter of biology. Regardless of accomplishment, religious practice or social stature, Jewish genetics predetermined the individual and his progeny to treachery and inferiority, Nazis believed. Hence, there were no "good Jews." They were all despicable "subhumans." Those with Jewish blood, even one drop from a grandparent, were reviled enemies of the Nazi state.

Many loyal Germans, even vigorous Nazi stalwarts or pious Christians, were completely unaware that somewhere in their background there might lurk a Jewish ancestor. Some 600,000 Jews had been identified in Germany since the first Nazi census in 1933. These individuals were clearly identified with the Jewish community, whether by religious, social, or cultural affiliations. But in his paranoia, *der Führer* suspected that the German nation was actually "infected" with more than two million individuals of partial Jewish descent. All these people would have to be identified and dealt with—and cleansed away as soon as possible.

Just who was a Jew? The answer to that question would define existence for millions under Nazi rule. The decision would be dictated by Nazi genetic science, adopted by Nazi regulation and enforced with brutal Nazi efficiency.

Under the Nuremberg Laws enacted in 1935 and later decrees, the elusive definitions were finally established. "Full Jews" were descended from three Jewish grandparents, or two Jewish parents. From there, all sorts of damning genetic fractions were calculated, such as *half-Jews* and *quarter-Jews*, depending upon the degree of Jewish lineage going back three generations. In many Reich circles, theorists propounded even more victimizing formulae, classifying some individuals as *sixteenth-Jews* and even *thirty-second-Jews.*

Those branded fully or partially as Jews were forbidden from interacting with Germans on any level—social or commercial—and required to progressively relinquish all rights and property. Beyond civil rights and entitlements, those marked as Jews were targeted for forced surgical sterilization to stop their blood lines, as well as expulsion and concentration. Eventually, Jews were subjected to lethal countermeasures to subtract their very existence. While full Jews were mercilessly persecuted, abused and murdered, those with a percentage of German blood were often decreed a measure of moderation allowing them to escape with their lives. But even those with a mere trace of Jewish blood were often forcibly sterilized to halt their lineage.

Who was allowed to live and thrive? Hitler worshipped the idealized white, blond, blue-eyed Aryan as a model human being. Through careful breeding and multiplication of Aryan stock, and the systematic elimination of all others—Jews and Gypsies first—

the Nazis hoped to create a new world order controlled by biologically dominant Germans. This was Hitler's notion of "the Master Race." The concept was just that, a genetically endowed superior race determined to become master of the world.

Nervous genealogy became the national obsession in Germany as ordinary Aryans scrambled to prove the purity of their ancestry going back three generations. It was literally a matter of life or death. To this end, race bureaus, investigators and tribunals were established throughout Germany. Methods of documenting family trees were as formal as hereditary court hearings complete with grandiose evidentiary exhibits to establish human pedigree, and as slippery as mean-spirited compilations of gossip and pure suspicion by quasi-official Nazi party offices.

Business competitors sued to prove which company had the right to advertise pure Aryan ownership. A flurry of terrified spouses from mixed Christian-Jewish marriages swore to genetic courts that their children were not the offspring of a Jewish parent, but rather the bastards of an Aryan tryst—thus preserving the ability of sons and daughters to escape anti-Jewish measures. Not a few Aryans were paid well to confirm that they fathered out-of-wedlock children.

German race policies were implemented not only in Germany but in every town and village across Europe that came under Nazi occupation. Racial bureaus were set up through Nazi Europe to identify, trace and evaluate who was a Jew and who was not, who could live and who should die, and under what conditions. Those with pure German blood were prized and salvaged from occupied nations. Others were to be brutally enslaved or mass murdered.

Hitler's maniacal and murderous raceology was based on a bizarre pseudo-science called *eugenics*. The German word for eugenics was *Rassenhygiene*, that is, "racial hygiene." The German and American terms became interchangeable in both countries.

Eugenics dominated everything the Third Reich did—who was plundered and who did the plundering, who was murdered and who did the murdering. Hence, Hitler's war against humanity was more than just a war of territorial conquest or economic expropriation. His was a "biological war," backed up by a genocidal military; a ruthless crusade to genetically purify the world and catapult the Master Race to its rightful dominion over mankind.

As Hitler's divisions smashed across Europe, the German eugenic ideal would be enforced against those in captured or dominated nations. In country after country, Hitler rounded up the Jews and other so-called subhumans, systematically making one region after another *judenrein*—Jew free.

As Hitler's deputy Rudolf Hess insisted, "National Socialism is nothing but applied biology."

Where did Hitler get his ghastly ideas about eugenics, bloodline percentages and genocidal scientific countermeasures to be waged in a war against those perceived inferior? Answer: From a group of corporate interests led by the Carnegie Institution, the Rockefeller Foundation and the Harriman railroad fortune—and the entrenched American laws that group labored so hard to achieve.

Eugenics began, almost naively, in 1863, when Sir Francis Galton, cousin of Charles Darwin, theorized that if talented people only married other talented people, the result would be measurably better, more talented offspring. Galton coined the term "eugenics" from Greek roots meaning "well," and "born," scribbling the new word on a small scrap of paper in his laboratory. Later, Galton propounded his theories into elaborate treatises and articles, attempting to find a mathematical method to predict which couples could be expected to yield the best offspring. Fundamentally, Galtonian eugenics was a credo of marriage management and planned procreation designed to improve society. In fact, it was an overly active cogitator's attempt to add predictive mathematics to the common familial wish: "marry well."

This wish turned into a monster.

At the turn of the last century, Galton's uncodified ideas were imported into the United States. At about the same time, Gregor Mendel's principles of heredity were rediscovered. American eugenic advocates believed with near religious fervor that Mendelian concepts explaining the color and size of peas, corn, and cattle also governed the social and intellectual character of man.

In the early twentieth century, America was reeling from the upheaval of massive immigration and torn by post-Reconstruction chaos. Race conflict was everywhere. Elitists, utopians and so-called "progressives" fused their smoldering race fears and class bias to their desire to make a better world, reinventing Galton's eugenics as a repressive and racist ideology. The new American eugenics saw such traits as poverty, prostitution, alcoholism, and criminality as genetically transmitted from generation to generation. You weren't born into poverty. Poverty was born into you. Ethnic and racial minorities were biologically predisposed to poverty, illiteracy, larceny, shiftlessness, and a spectrum of other social failings. One could never rise above adverse social circumstances. The flaws in your blood would eventually bring you down. With utopian myopia, eugenicists believed by eliminating the physical existence of minorities, the social ills of society would eventually disappear. To this end, American eugenicists were determined to populate the earth with vastly more of their own socioeconomic and biological kind, and fewer—or none—of everyone else.

Who did they want? The superior species the eugenics movement sought was not merely tall, strong and talented. American eugenicists craved those that resembled their own forefathers: blond, blue-eyed "Nordic" types. This group alone, they believed, was fit to inherit the earth.

In the process, American eugenicists intended to subtract blacks, Indians, Hispanics, Eastern Europeans, Jews, dark-haired hillbillies, poor people, the infirm—essentially, anyone outside the gentrified genetic lines drawn up by American race theory.

How would they do it? By identifying so-called "defective" family trees and subjecting them to lifelong segregation and sterilization programs to kill off their bloodlines. The grand plan was literally to wipe away the reproductive capability and continued existence of the "unfit"— those deemed weak and inferior. Their assets would be seized to repay society for the many hospitals and prisons required to house and accommodate them.

Eighteen solutions to the world's genetic pollution were explored in a 1911 Carnegie-supported study titled "Preliminary Report of the Committee of the Eugenic Section of the American Breeder's Association to Study and to Report on the Best Practical Means for Cutting Off the Defective Germ-Plasm in the Human Population."

The most commonly suggested method of eugenicide in America was the "lethal chamber," that is, a network of publicly located and operated gas chambers.

In 1918, Paul Popenoe, a U.S. Army venereal disease specialist during World War I, co-wrote the widely used textbook, *Applied Eugenics*, which argued, "From an historical point of view, the first method which presents itself is execution... Its value in keeping up the standard of the race should not be underestimated." *Applied Eugenics* also devoted a chapter to "Lethal Selection," which operated "through the destruction of the individual by some adverse feature of the environment, such as excessive cold, or bacteria, or by bodily deficiency."

Eugenic breeders believed American society was not ready to implement an organized and orderly mass extermination of its own citizenry. But many mental institutions and doctors practiced improvised medical lethality and passive euthanasia anyway. For example, one institution in Lincoln, Illinois fed its incoming patients milk from tubercular cows, believing a eugenically strong individual would be immune. Thirty to forty percent annual death rates resulted at Lincoln. Other doctors at mental institutions engaged in lethal neglect to quietly accomplish a similar result. Some doctors practiced passive eugenicide one newborn infant at a time. In 1915, Chicago doctor Harry Haiselden became famous as "the Black Stork," making Hollywood movies and touring widely for proudly killing defective babies he deemed "unworthy of life."

Nonetheless, with eugenicide marginalized, the main solution for eugenicists was the rapid expansion of forced segregation and sterilization, as well as more marriage restrictions. California in 1909 became the third state in the country to adopt eugenic legislation. Leading the nation in eugenic action, California performed nearly all its involuntary sterilization procedures with little or no due process. In its first twenty-five years of eugenic legislation, California sterilized 9,782 individuals, mostly women. The practice continued unabated for decades.

In 1933 alone, at least 1,278 coercive sterilizations were performed in California, 700 of which were on women. The state's two leading sterilization mills in 1933 were Sonoma State Home with 388 operations and Patton State Hospital with 363 operations. Other sterilization centers included Agnews, Mendocino, Napa, Norwalk, Stockton and Pacific Colony state hospitals. Many victims were classified as "bad girls," diagnosed as "passionate," "oversexed" or "sexually wayward." At the Sonoma State Home, some women were sterilized because of what was deemed an abnormally large clitoris or labia.

California was considered an epicenter of the American eugenics movement. During the twentieth century's first decades, California's eugenicists included potent, even if little known, race scientists, such as Army venereal disease specialist Popenoe, citrus magnate and Polytechnic benefactor Paul Gosney, and Sacramento banker Charles M. Goethe, as well as members of the California State Board of Charities and Corrections and the University of California Board of Regents.

Where California led, many states followed. Indiana, Connecticut and Virginia adopted some of the most vigorous eugenic programs to do away with family bloodlines. Eventually, 27 states enacted eugenic laws.

Ultimately, at least 60,000 Americans were coercively sterilized—legally and extra legally. Many never discovered the truth until decades later. Thousands more were incarcerated in camps or colonies because their shy or non-verbal demeanor was deemed "defective." Sometimes too much smile on their face qualified them as simpletons. Almost always, it was because the victims were poor.

Untold additional thousands more were prohibited from being married or were administratively "unmarried" because of ethnic intermarriage prohibited by law. Virginia's Racial Integrity Act was the nation's paramount example of a racist marriage prohibition disguised as eugenic science. Racist eugenicist Walter Plecker, the state's registrar, waged a one-man reign of bureaucratic terror to stop the admixing of the races in Virginia. He enforced the state's "one-drop" rule, meaning that even one drop of non-white blood in a person's distant ancestry made him a Negro—barring them from marrying whites, and from the benefits of white schooling and progressive society. Draconian racial checking of all births, marriages and deaths, as well as brazen intimidation tactics, allowed Plecker to nullify many marriages and prevent numberless others—all in the name of proven science.

A leading Virginia racist and eugenicist, John Powell, explained his state's inter-racial marriage eugenic prohibitions in these words: "Of course, laws against intermarriage cannot solve the Negro problem in any of its aspects—industrial, economic, political, social, biological or eugenical. They can, however, delay the evil day and give time for the evolvement of an effective solution... a real and final solution." Virginia eugenicists were determined to wipe out more than Blacks. They also wanted to do away with Indians, mixed-race families and poor whites—a group that state officials collectively called "Mongrel Virginians." In fact, the state actually published an official reference pamphlet entitled *Mongrel Virginians* to expound on the issue.

Elite academics participated as full partners in the repression. Psychiatrists and psychologists, for example, invented racist mental testing programs to scientifically identify those targeted for ethnic extinction. During the World War I period, Americans and naturalized immigrants at Ellis Island who could neither read nor write English were administered picture exams known as the Beta Test. Designed to confuse, Beta Test 6 for example, offered 20 simple sketches with something missing. "Fix it," the subject was instructed. The tested person was then expected to pencil in the missing element. Bowling balls were missing from a bowling lane. The center net was subtracted from a tennis court. The incandescent filament was erased from a light bulb. A stamp was missing from a postcard. Naturally, in those early twentieth century days, many rural or immigrant individuals with great intelligence had never bowled, played tennis, purchased a light bulb or mailed a postcard. The Alpha Test employed trick questions to ask poor rural people or immigrants to identify pop culture such as tobacco brands and advertising campaigns they had never been exposed to.

Alpha and Beta tests proved to scientists that 47 percent of whites generally, 70 percent of Jews and 89 percent of Negroes were deserving of eugenic elimination. The technical term *moron* was coined. This eugenic system was refined into what is today known as the intelligence quotient or "IQ."

The surgical, agricultural, anthropology and sociology professions all combined to create the vogue, sham science of the day—eugenics. Even ophthalmologists assumed a leading role in the persecution. Led by pioneer eye doctor Lucien Howe, ophthalmologists hatched a macabre plan whereby people with a range of eye problems and their families would be offered the option of being isolated in camps or sterilized. "A large part, if not all, of this misery and expense," promised Howe, "could be gradually eradicated by sequestration or by sterilization, if the transmitter of the defect preferred the later." Howe suggested that authorities wait to discover a visually-impaired person, and then go back and get the rest of her or his family. In 1921, enabling legislation was drafted by the New York State legislature with the help of Columbia University attorneys, but New York State Bill #1597 did not pass. But many other laws in many other states did pass, creating a patchwork of medical repression.

Even the United States Supreme Court endorsed eugenics as national policy. In an infamous 1927 decision based on an obviously collusive court case, *Buck v. Bell*, Supreme Court Justice Oliver Wendell Holmes juridically enshrined the government's right to sterilize and end blood lines of those deemed "unfit." The test case involved Virginia's effort to complete the sterilization of Carrie Buck, as well as her mother, and daughter as "degenerates." Holmes wrote, "It is better for all the world, if instead of waiting to execute degenerate offspring for crime, or to let them starve for their imbecility, society can prevent those who are manifestly unfit from continuing their kind... Three generations of imbeciles are enough."

Eugenics would have been so much bizarre parlor talk had it not been for extensive financing by corporate philanthropies, specifically the Carnegie Institution that arose from industrial steel, the Rockefeller Foundation, born of an oil monopoly, and the robber baron Harriman fortune, built by railroads. They were all in league with some of America's most respected scientists hailing from such prestigious universities as Stanford, Yale, Harvard, and Princeton. These academicians espoused race theory and race science, and then faked and twisted the data to serve the movement's racist aims. Eugenic science was bought and paid for by the elite for the elite to perpetrate a genetic war against everyone else. Corporate money powered it all.

In 1904, the Carnegie Institution allocated large grants to establish a laboratory complex at Cold Spring Harbor on Long Island. Heading up the Cold Spring Harbor network was its stern-faced, Puritan-minded director Charles Davenport. With Carnegie Institution money and approval, Davenport created an interlocking group of eugenic entities.

First, in 1904, he founded the Station for Experimental Evolution to develop the science of eugenics, including a library, seminars, and the initiation of journals. From there, researchers could carefully plot the removal of families, bloodlines and whole peoples. Cold Spring Harbor eugenics advocates, all under Carnegie funding, agitated in the legislatures of America, as well as the nation's social service agencies and associations. The Harriman railroad fortune paid local charities, such as the New York Bureau of Industries and Immigration, to seek out Jewish, Italian and other immigrants in New York and other crowded cities and subject them to deportation, trumped-up confinement or forced sterilization.

In 1910, using Carnegie resources and money contributed by the Harriman railroad fortune, Davenport added a Eugenics Record Office (ERO). Davenport's designated tactician Harry Laughlin was appointed to head up the office. The ERO's mission was to quietly register the genetic backgrounds of all Americans, separating the defective strains from the desired lineages. The self-aggrandizing Laughlin borrowed nomenclature and charting procedures from the world of animal breeding, inflating every concept into a tenet of social engineering. Family trees would be called *pedigrees* to be analyzed and judged like those of a dog or a horse.

Where would the ERO obtain the family details? "They lie hidden," Davenport told his ABA colleagues, "in records of our numerous charity organizations, our 42 institutions for the feeble-minded, our 115 schools and homes for the deaf and blind, our 350 hospitals for the insane, our 1,200 refuge homes, our 1,300 prisons, our 1,500 hospitals and our 2,500 almshouses. Our great insurance companies and our college gymnasiums have tens of thousands of records of the characters of human bloodlines. These records should be studied, their hereditary data sifted out and properly recorded on cards, and [then] the cards sent to a central bureau for study... [of] the great strains of human protoplasm that are coursing through the country."

At the same time, Davenport wanted the ERO to collect pedigrees on eminent, racially acceptable families, that is, the ones worth preserving.

The Carnegie complex also helped found the Eugenics Research Association to coordinate the efforts of eugenicists across the nation. A publication, *Eugenical News*, published out of the ERO offices, served the entire field with regular updates. Together, the ERO, *Eugenical News*, and the Carnegie Station wielded an army of field workers, researchers, theorists and affiliated local organizations to assemble a web of gossip and fake science to justify racial regulation.

The goal: ethnically cleanse millions of people—10 percent at a time. When the work began, the initial goal was to subtract 14 million Americans, the so-called "lower tenth." When that genetically defective layer was gone, race partisans intended to slice away a tenth of the remainder, repeating the process over and over again until no one was left standing but those that resembled the blond-haired, blue-eyed Nordic stereotype American eugenics worshipped.

Naturally, the work of eugenics was devoted to ethnic cleansing in the United States. But waves of immigration made the genetically impure world beyond America's shore just as important. Preventing the inferior overseas from reaching America would be the first line of defense. Understandable, Germany, rich in blond, blue-eyed citizens, constituted a treasured region for American eugenicists. Germany was the country to both emulate and help purify.

Hitler's arrival on the eugenic scene changed the entire partnership between German and American eugenicists. During the first two decades of the twentieth century, America had shown Germany the way, treating the struggling German movement with both parental fascination and Nordic admiration. But when Hitler emerged in 1924, the relationship quickly shifted to an equal partnership.

National Socialism promised a sweeping hereditary revolution, establishing dictatorial racial procedures that American activists could only dream of. During the period between wars, the American movement viewed National Socialism as a rising force that could successfully, if empowered, impose a new biological world order. Nazi eugenicists promised to dispense with the niceties of democratic rule.

So even if America's tower of legislation, well-funded research and entrenched bureaucratic programs still monopolized the world of applied eugenics in the 1920s, National Socialism promised to own the next decade. American eugenicists welcomed the idea. Therefore, during the 1920s, Carnegie Institution eugenics scientists cultivated deep personal and professional relationships with Germany's fascist eugenicists. Many of these eugenicists would graduate to become the killing doctors of the Third Reich.

As early as 1923, Davenport and Laughlin decided that *Eugenical News* should add a subtitle to its name. It became *Eugenical News: Current Record of Race Hygiene*. In doing so, the publication discarded any pretense that it might be anything other than a race science journal. Adding Germany's unique term for eugenics, *race hygiene*, was also a bow by the American movement to the Germans.

Soon, articles from the German journal *Archiv für Rassen- und Gesellschaftsbiologie* (*Archives of Race Science and Social Biology*) were highlighted and summarized almost quarterly in *Eugenical News*. In fact, no longer did such reviews bear specific headlines about interesting articles. Rather, the summaries appeared as though they were regular columns, often just headlined "Archiv für Rassen- und Gesellschaftsbiologie," as the contents of the German journal's latest issue were explored. Articles by German raceologists Erwin Baur, Eugen Fischer and Fritz Lenz were among those most frequently featured. While all three espoused anti-Jewish biological views, the latter two became among the most notorious lab-coated commandants of Hitler's murderous science.

In the 1920s, German raceologists became even more sought after as authors and topics for both *Eugenical News* and another American scientific publication, *Journal of Heredity*. As their names appeared more frequently in American publications, the German influence over American eugenic circles only increased. For instance, in May of 1924, Lenz authored a long article for the *Journal of Heredity* simply titled "Eugenics in Germany," with the latest news and historical reminiscences. California eugenicist Popenoe, who also headed up the rabidly eugenic Human Betterment Foundation, functioned as Lenz's principal translator in the United States. Similar articles were published from time to time as updates, thus keeping the American movement's attention riveted on the vicissitudes of the German school. A typically enthralled review of the latest German booklet on race hygiene ran in the October 1924 *Eugenical News* with the lead sentence: "It was a happy thought that led Dr. Lewellys F. Barker, a leading eugenicist as well as a physician, to translate the little book of Dr. H.W. Siemens, of Munich, into English." Such fawning editorial treatment for German race hygiene appeared in virtually every edition of American eugenic journals.

Nor was coverage of German race hygienists and their work limited to the eugenic press. Developments were reported as legitimate medical news in almost every issue of the *Journal of the American Medical Association*, chiefly by the journal's German correspondent. For example, in May of 1924, Baur's latest lecture to Berlin's local eugenics society was covered in great detail in a two-column story. *JAMA* repeated, without comment or qualification, Baur's blatant race politics. "A person of moderate gifts may be educated to be very efficient," the article read, "but he will never transmit other than moderate gifts to his own offspring. The attempts to elevate the negroes of the United States by giving them the same educational advantages the white population receives have necessarily failed." The *JAMA* article also regurgitated Baur's contention that a controversial book chronicling the fabricated family history of a clan pseudonymously named "The Jukes" was proof positive of eugenically damaged ancestry. "Race suicide," *JAMA* continued from Baur's speech, "brought about the downfall of Greece and Rome, and Germany is confronted by the same peril." *JAMA* presented the statements as unqualified, well-settled medical knowledge.

Nor did the meteoric rise of Hitler in Weimar hate politics, after 1924, diminish the frequency or prominence of German raceologists' exposure in the American eugenic press. The January 1926 issue of *Eugenical News* featured a long article, written by Lenz, titled "Are the Gifted Families in America Maintaining Themselves?" Dense with smoked statistics and formulas, Lenz's article analyzed recent California eugenic research with a German mindset, warning "the dying out of the gifted families... of the North American Union [United States] proceeds not less rapidly; and also among us in Europe... I think one ought not to look at the collapse of the best elements of the race without action."

A linchpin in the American-German möbius was Lehmanns Verlag, Germany's foremost eugenic publishing house. Lehmanns published the translated work of many American eugenic theorists, as well as original German eugenic tomes. Julius Lehmann was not just a publisher with a proclivity for race biology. He had been a shoulder-to-shoulder co-conspirator with Hitler during the 1923 Beer Hall Putsch, and was at Hitler's side on November 8, 1923, when the National Socialists launched their abortive coup against the Bavarian government. After the beer hall ruckus, Bavarian officials were held hostage at Lehmann's ornate villa until the uprising was suppressed. As the revolt collapsed, Lehmann, a financial supporter as well as a friend, convinced the Nazi guards to allow their captives to escape rather than execute them. Lehmann was the intellectual connection between the theory of Germany's racist Society for Racial Hygiene and the biological mindsets of such militants as the Nazis.

It was no accident that Hitler read the monumental German eugenic reference, *Foundation of Human Heredity and Race Hygiene* authored by Baur, Fisher and Lenz. Lehmanns Verlag published it. Indeed, someone at Lehmanns happily reported to Lenz that Hitler had read his book. Lehmanns Verlag also published *Archiv für Rassen- und Gesellschaftsbiologie* by the father of German raceology, the American-trained Alfred Ploetz. The firm also published *Monatsschrift für Kriminalbiologie (Monthly Journal of Criminal Biology)*. One of the most popular volumes published by Lehmanns Verlag was von Hoffmann's *Racial Hygiene in the United States*. The year after Hitler was imprisoned, Lehmanns published the German translation of American eugenicist Madison Grant's bestselling volume, *The Passing of the Great Race*, which had a profound effect on Hitler's thinking.

Lehmanns Verlag was in regular, mutually supportive contact with the Cold Spring Harbor group. When Lehmanns released a series of "race cards," that is, popular trading cards depicting racial profiles—from the Tamils of India to the primitive Baskirs of the Ural Mountains, their availability was fondly reported in *Eugenical News*. Fascinated with the novelty, *Eugenical News* suggested, however, that the cards could be improved if the pictures would reveal more body features. German race cards, just like many baseball cards, came 10 to a package.

As the German movement grew more virulent, its esteem in American eugenic circles only rose. Its pronouncements became more authoritative. Unchallenged and unquestioned German racial references to Jews gradually became commonplace in American publications. For example, in the April 1924 issue of *Eugenical News*, an article reviewing a new German "racial pride" book published by Lehmanns mentioned, "In an appendix the Jews are considered, their history and their role in Germany." A German article on consanguineous marriages summarized in the November 1925 issue of *Eugenical News* stated, "Their evil consequences… are pointed out [and]… are commoner among Jews and royalty than elsewhere in the population."

German race analyses of American society were always well received. In May of 1927, *Eugenical News* reported the introduction of a German "race biological index," to eugenically rate different ethnic groups for value to mankind. The article repeated German warnings "of the danger of an eruption of colored races over Europe, through the French colonies [in Africa] and colonial troops." In the article, German researchers urged "further studies in America, both of Indians and American negroes, as compared with those still living in Africa."

A December 1927 summary of a German article reported, "The social biology and social hygiene of the Jew is treated by the distinguished anthropologist, Wissenberg of Ukrania. This has largely to do with the vital statistics of the Jews in Odessa and Elizabethgrad, with special relation of the Jews to acute infection." In April 1929, a *Eugenical News* book review entitled "Noses and Ears" informed readers, "The straight nose of Gentiles seems to dominate over the convex nose of Jews." No explanation was necessary or offered for these out-of-context references to Jews. That Jews were eugenically undesirable was a "given" in German eugenics, and many American eugenicists adopted that view as well.

By the mid-twenties, Germany had achieved preeminence in both legitimate genetic research and spurious racial biology. Germany's new status arose, in large measure, from its distinguished Kaiser Wilhelm Institutes. An outgrowth of the esteemed Kaiser Wilhelm Society, the Kaiser Wilhelm Institutes would, over time, develop a network of research institutions devoted to the highest pursuits of science. These included the Kaiser Wilhelm Institute for Physics, boasting a staff of Nobel Prize winners, a sister institute for chemistry, another for biology, one for pathology and on through the leading scientific disciplines. The twenty-plus Kaiser Wilhelm organizations were easily confused and bore related names. But while they were nominally related, they were actually independent and often located in different cities. At one point Davenport confessed to a London colleague, "There are so many Kaiser Wilhelm Institutes, that it is necessary to specify."

Several Kaiser Wilhelm Institutes significantly contributed to basic science. But among the Kaiser Wilhelm Institutes were also several that would soon make their mark in the history of medical murder. The first was the Kaiser Wilhelm Institute for Psychiatry. The second was the Institute for Anthropology, Human Heredity and Eugenics. The third was the Institute for Brain Research. All received funding and administrative support from Americans, especially the Rockefeller Foundation.

Indeed, the Rockefeller Foundation helped found the German eugenics program itself. The corporate philanthropy built key eugenic laboratories from the ground up, paid for scientific studies, subsidized travel, financed journals and publication, and extended lucrative fellowships to German eugenicists—all to continue research into America's racist notions of biology. The fruits of this research were to be implemented in Europe.

By 1926, Rockefeller had donated some $410,000—almost $4 million in today's dollars—to hundreds of German researchers. In May 1926, for example, Rockefeller awarded $250,000 to the German Psychiatric Institute of the Kaiser Wilhelm Institute, which became the Kaiser Wilhelm Institute for Psychiatry. Among the leading psychiatrists at the German Psychiatric Institute was Ernst Rüdin, who became its director, and eventually an architect of Hitler's systematic medical repression.

Another in the Kaiser Wilhelm Institute's complex of eugenic establishments was the Institute for Brain Research. Since 1915, the Institute for Brain Research had operated out of a single room. But everything changed when Rockefeller money arrived in 1929. A grant of $317,000 allowed the institute to construct a major building and take center stage in German race biology. During the next several years, the Institute for Brain Research received additional grants from the Rockefeller Foundation.

Leading the Brain Institute was—once again—Hitler's medical henchman, Rüdin.

Rüdin, of course, was quite visible in America. Articles by and about him had run in the national eugenic press for years. In May of 1922, the *Journal of Heredity* published a brief about a Rüdin talk on the inheritance of mental defects. In June of 1924, *Eugenical News* informed its readership that Rüdin was building an extensive collection of family histories, and assured "a vast quantity of data has been obtained." Later that year, in the September issue, *Eugenical News* published a follow-up report, asserting that Rüdin's studies of the "inheritance of mental disorders are the most thorough that are being undertaken anywhere. It is hoped that they will be long continued and expanded." A 1925 *Eugenical News* article praising the family tree archives of the German Psychiatric Institute, celebrated Rüdin, "whose dynamic personality infuses itself throughout the entire establishment." By this time, Rüdin was the star of German eugenics. Even the *Journal of the American Medical Association* published a long report about Rüdin's work on heredity and mental disease.

Rüdin's organization became a prime director and beneficiary of murderous experimentation and research conducted on Jews, Gypsies and others. Beginning in 1940, thousands of Germans taken from old age homes, mental institutions and other custodial facilities were systematically gassed. In all, between 50,000 and 100,000 were killed.

"While we were pussy-footing around," said Leon Whitney, executive secretary of the American Eugenics Society, "the Germans were calling a spade a spade."

In 1924, when Hitler wrote *Mein Kampf*, he frequently quoted American eugenic ideology and openly displayed a thorough knowledge of American eugenics and its phraseology. "There is today one state," Hitler wrote, "in which at least weak beginnings toward a better conception [of immigration] are noticeable. Of course, it is not our model German Republic, but the United States." Hitler proudly told his comrades just how closely he followed American eugenic legislation. "I have studied with great interest the laws of several American states concerning prevention of reproduction by people whose progeny would, in all probability, be of no value or be injurious to the racial stock," he told a fellow Nazi. Hitler merely exchanged the American term "Nordic" for "Germanic" or "Aryan" and then medicalized his pre-existing virulent anti-Semitism and fascist nationalism, to formulate the concept of the Master Race he deified in *Mein Kampf*.

Der Führer's rallying cry was *Rasse und blut*! Race and blood. Bloodline determined all that was physically and socially worthy of existence, he insisted. Everything to be exalted or exterminated had a genetic quotient. But it was Stanford University president David Starr Jordan, a eugenic pioneer, who had originated the notion of "race and blood" in his 1902 racial epistle, *Blood of a Nation*. In that book, the university scholar declared that human qualities and conditions such as talent and poverty were passed through the blood, generation to generation, as a racial trait.

Hitler was so steeped in American race science, he even wrote a fan letter to American eugenic leader Madison Grant. *Der Führer's* letter called Grant's eugenics book, *The Passing of the Great Race*, "my bible."

Race science, racial purity and racial dominance powered Hitler's Nazism. American theories were implemented by Hitler with great ferocity and velocity, exceeding anything the Americans could imagine. Nazi doctors would become the unseen generals in Hitler's war against the Jews and other Europeans deemed inferior. Doctors would devise the eugenic formulas, and even hand-selected the victims for sterilization, euthanasia or mass extermination. Black shirts and brown shirts would inflict the horror—but white coats directed it.

Much of the spiritual guidance and political agitation for the American eugenics movement came from California's quasi-autonomous eugenic societies, such as the Pasadena-based Human Betterment Foundation and the California branch of the American Eugenics Society, which coordinated much of their activity with the eugenics headquarters on Long Island. These organizations— which functioned as part of a closely-knit network—published racist eugenic newsletters and pseudo-scientific journals that resonated with Nazi precepts. The groups and their publications eagerly propagandized in America for the Nazis.

In 1927, the Kaiser Wilhelm Institutes added another eugenic establishment, the Institute for Anthropology, Human Heredity and Eugenics (*Kaiser Wilhelm Institut für Anthropologie, menschliche Erblehre und Eugenik*), located in Berlin-Dahlem. The name itself symbolized the affinity between the American and German movements. Earlier, *Eugenical News* had adopted a subtitle in homage to the German term *race hygiene*; now the Kaiser Wilhelm Institutes reciprocated by including the term *eugenics* in tribute to the American movement.

The first director of the Institute for Anthropology, Human Heredity and Eugenics was Eugen Fischer, the longtime Carnegie Institution associate, Davenport collaborator and rabid Nazi raceologist. This new institute was not funded by American capital, but rather by an assortment of German government agencies—local, Prussian and federal—to whom eugenics and race science were becoming increasingly important. The Ministry of the Interior provided the largest single donation: 500,000 marks. The Prussian Ministry of Science donated some 400,000 marks, including the land itself. Small amounts were also contributed by the provinces of Upper Silesia, the Rhine, Westphalia and the municipality of Essen. Funds from industrialists, such as the Thyssen brothers, added token money. While the institute's initial funding was German, it enjoyed both the envy and unqualified support of the American eugenics establishment.

The grand opening of the Institute for Anthropology, Human Heredity and Eugenics took place in September of 1927 as an official function of the Fifth International Congress on Genetics in Berlin. Davenport was chairman of the human eugenics program and an honorary president of the congress. Baur was chairman of the local German eugenics committee. The congress was the first major international scientific event to be held in Germany since the Great War. America's contingent had pushed for the German venue.

On September 11, 1927, the Fifth International Congress on Genetics began with approximately one thousand delegates from all over the world gathered in a gala Berlin setting. Registrants were first greeted with a Sunday dinner at the Berlin Zoo, then a barrage of sumptuous banquets staged by the Berlin Municipality and formal dinner events enlivened by *divertimenti*, followed by the finest liquors and cigars. Museum tours were scheduled for the ladies, and everyone was invited to a special performance at the Opera House. Germany was unfurling the red carpet to celebrate its regained scientific leadership, a niche restored thanks to the protracted assist by American corporate philanthropies.

Welcoming grandiloquence by both government officials and local academics eventually gave way to the real business of the Berlin conference: genetics. A procession of several dozen research papers and exhibits circulated the latest developments in a spectrum of related disciplines, from genuine scientific revelations about the genetics of plants and animals, to the most recent advances in cytology, to the newest slogans and Mendelian math of traditional racial eugenics. A large Carnegie delegation was on hand to contribute its own research, proffering papers and delivering lectures.

On the afternoon of September 27, 1927, Davenport and his colleagues traveled to Berlin-Dahlem for the much-anticipated grand opening of the new Institute for Anthropology, Human Heredity and Eugenics. Situated on about an acre of land, with a museum in the basement and a complex of lecture rooms, measurement labs and libraries on most other floors, the institute was the new centerpiece of eugenic research in Germany. From the moment he had learned about Fischer's appointment almost a year earlier, Davenport had been eager to congratulate his friend in person. As the leader of American eugenics, Davenport proudly delivered one of the commemorating addresses at the grand opening.

Another pivotal Kaiser Wilhelm Institute was the Institute for Brain Research. This one grew out of a research operation created years earlier by the family of psychiatrist Oskar Vogt, which merged into the Kaiser Wilhelm Institute in 1915. In those days, the Institute for Brain Research was housed in Vogt's modest neurological laboratory. Everything changed when the Rockefeller money arrived in 1929. A grant of $317,000—a fortune during the Depression—allowed the institute to construct a major building and take center stage in German race biology. Rockefeller funders were especially interested in the Institute's Department of Experimental Genetics. The Institute for Brain Research received additional grants from the Rockefeller Foundation during the next several years.

By the late twenties, Davenport and other Americans had created a whirlwind of joint projects and entanglements with German eugenics. No longer content to merely direct purely domestic efforts in their countries, the two schools now eyed the rest of the world. They graduated from discussion and philosophy to concrete plans and actions. Among the most ambitious of these was a project to identify and subject to eugenic measures every individual of mixed race--everywhere. The approach would be along the lines created in the United States. Identification was the first step. In 1927, Davenport proposed a systematic survey of mixed-race populations in every region of the world. The survey would cover all Africans, Europeans, Asians, Mexicans, indigenous peoples and any others who had mixed during centuries of modern civilization.

The global search for "hybrids" had originated around February of 1926. Davenport had made the acquaintance of wealthy raceologist Wickliffe Draper, who shared Davenport's anxiety about human hybridization. The plan was to conduct field surveys using questionnaires, just as eugenicists had done in various counties and remote areas around the United States. But this time, the effort would cover not just a state, not just a nation, but eventually every populated region on earth. They selected Jamaica as a testbed. The plan, embodied in the Carnegie-sponsored Jamaica Race-Crossing Project, was to catalog every Jamaican—this as the first step in eliminating the existence of Africans on earth.

As part of its international thrust, Carnegie propagandized and promoted Nazi science globally. Davenport was more than successful in bringing the Germans, ostracized after their World War

I defeat, back into the international eugenics movement. In 1928, the International Federation of Eugenic Organizations (IFEO) met in Munich, following a Cold Spring Harbor push to meet in Germany. Rüdin functioned as the gracious host when IFEO members, including the impressed American delegation, were treated to a guided tour of Rüdin's department at the Kaiser Wilhelm Institute for Psychiatry. The next year, the Kaiser Wilhelm Institute for Psychiatry was selected for IFEO membership. In 1932, Davenport consented to relinquish the presidency of the IFEO, and Rüdin was elected to succeed him. Davenport's assistant, Laughlin, of the Eugenic Record Office was proud to offer the nomination. The vote was unanimous. German race hygiene was now primed to seize the reins of the international movement and become senior in its partnership with the American branch.

Indeed, during the Reich's first decade of power, dazzled American eugenicists welcomed Hitler's plans as the logical fulfillment of their own decades of research and effort. Ten years after Virginia passed its 1924 sterilization act, Joseph DeJarnette, superintendent of Virginia's Western State Hospital, complained in the *Richmond Times-Dispatch*, "The Germans are beating us at our own game." In 1934, sterilizations in Germany were accelerating beyond 5,000 per month, dwarfing America's program.

In 1935, when Hitler demanded a definition of just who was a full Jew, *half-Jew,* and *quarter-Jew*, the genetic formulas adopted were those devised by the Carnegie network, specifically those of ERO director Laughlin. During the mid to late 1920s, Laughlin spearheaded legislation in Congress to establish immigration quotas for Europeans based on the biological value of various ethnic groups. Southern Italians, Russians and many others were deemed to be genetically prone to the never-defined diagnosis of feeble-mindedness, as well as epilepsy, criminality, and laziness, among other derisive traits. Laughlin countered charges of bogus data and discrimination by appealing to eugenic sympathizers on the House Committee hearing his report, and by insisting that open immigration policies were already discriminating against one group: Nordics.

The House Committee tried to dress up the Carnegie testimony and exhibits by inventing a new federal title, "Expert Eugenics Agent" for Laughlin. House supporters hoped that this new title would add authority to any assertion Laughlin proffered.

Following up under the color of his new high-sounding status, "Expert Eugenics Agent," Laughlin dispatched an official Congressional publication to hundreds of state hospitals, prisons and other custodial institutions spread across the United States. The purpose: to trace the ancestry of all those under their care. The booklet was titled "Classification Standards to be Followed in Preparing Data for the Schedule 'Racial and Diagnostic Records of Inmates of State Institutions.'" Laughlin's title, "Expert Eugenics Agent," was printed on the cover. The booklet listed sixty-five racial classifications to be employed. Classification #15 was German Jew, #16 was Polish Jew, #17 was Russian Jew, #18 was Spanish-American (Indian), #19 was Spanish-American (White), #25 was North Italian, #26 was South Italian, #29 was Russian, #30 was Polish (Polack), #61 was Mountain White, #62 was American Yankee, #63 was American Southerner, and #64 was Middle West American. Crimes to be classified for genetic purposes included several dozen offenses ranging from homicide and arson to driving recklessly, disorderly conduct, and conducting business under an assumed name. The data collected would all go into one mammoth Mendelian database to help set race-based immigration quotas that Congress could adopt.

The Carnegie Institution was no bystander to Laughlin's operation. Laughlin regularly kept Carnegie President John Merriam briefed on his special Congressional privileges and the testing regimens placed at the disposal of the eugenics movement. Merriam authorized Carnegie statisticians to validate the reliability of the data Laughlin offered Congress.

However, Laughlin's derogatory race assertions were now becoming more public, and Merriam feared that his views would not be popular with America's vocal minorities. Indeed, by the mid-1920s, Laughlin and the Carnegie Institution were both being mocked by many educated people who saw eugenics as so much racial hokum. But Laughlin still had the ear of the powerful, racially motivated members of the House Committee. Congressional eagerness to adopt Laughlin's race-based immigration quotas only sparked more public ridicule, including in the media.

The irreverent *Baltimore Sun* commentator H. L. Mencken, or one of his associates, using the pseudonym "Ezekiel Cheever," began issuing sarcastic booklets on the subject under the name *School Issues*. In a "Special Extra Eugenics Number" Cheever "wickedly squeals on Doctor Harry H. Laughlin of the Carnegie Institution and other Members of the Eugenics Committee of the United States of America for feeding scientifically and biologically impure data to Honorable Members of the House of Representatives concerning the Immigration Problem." In page after page of satirical jabs, Laughlin's statistics were cited verbatim and then dismembered for their preposterousness.

For example, Cheever deprecated Laughlin's reliance on IQ testing, such as the Alpha and Beta exams, to gauge feeblemindedness. "Undoubtedly, one of the greatest blunders made by scientific men in America the past fifty years," Cheever wrote, "was the premature publication of the results of the Army [Alpha and Beta intelligence] tests." Mocking Laughlin's scientific racism, Cheever titled one section "Nigger in the Wood-Pile," which charged, "If the opinions advanced by Doctor Laughlin and based upon this same unscientific rubbish, are as unreliable as they appear when the rubbish is revealed in a true light, then it would seem that the Carnegie Institution of Washington must either disclaim any part of the job or confess that the job, despite Carnegie Institution's part, is a rotten one."

Cheever scolded "Honorable Albert Johnson, Chairman of the House's Committee on Immigration and Naturalization and a member of the Eugenics Committee, [who] announced at the hearings: 'I have examined Doctor Laughlin's data and charts and find that they are both biologically and statistically thorough, and apparently sound.' It is now in order for Congress to examine Honorable Albert Johnson and ascertain if as much can be said about him."

In a section titled "Naughty Germ Plasms," referring to Laughlin's race-based state institution surveys, Cheever jeered, "If the reader will examine the schedules sent out to cooperating institutions, he will get a new and somewhat startling view as to what constitutes 'the more serious crimes or felonies.' Under adult types of crime there were listed: Drunkenness, Conducting business under an assumed name, Peddling without license, Begging, and Reckless driving. Among the serious crimes or felonies of the juvenile type he will find: Trespass, Unlawful use of automobiles, Begging, Truancy, Running away, Being a stubborn and disobedient child. If Doctor Laughlin can devise a means for locating germ plasms that are responsible for such heinous crimes, his fame will overshadow that of Pasteur."

Often, the booklet used Laughlin's own words against him. Cheever quoted from one passage in Laughlin's testimony that confessed, "At the beginning of this investigation, there were in existence no careful or extended studies of this particular subject; the figures that were generally given were either guesswork or based upon very small samples of the population."

Cheever scorned, "Either Doctor Laughlin is exceedingly stupid, or else he is merely a statistical legerdemain [sleight of hand artist]."

Despite the mockery and the broad public outcry, which included denunciations from the growing mass of immigrant constituencies and their societies, Congress passed Laughlin's racial immigration quota legislation. Most referred to the legislation as the "National Origins Act." Several years later, the sham science, tortured formulae and flawed thinking that went into the National Origins Act were adopted as scientific fact by the Nazis.

When in 1935 Hitler demanded specific genetic fractions for Full Jew, half-Jew and quarter-Jew, the Nazis, of course, duplicated the race ancestry charts created by Laughlin and American eugenics. Carnegie racial math became the basis for the "the Laws for the Protection of German Blood and German Honor"—the Nuremberg Laws.

The new formulaic approach to Jewish persecution exploded

into world headlines. Under a page one banner story, the *New York Times*'s lead was typical: "National Socialist Germany definitely flung down the gauntlet before the feet of Western liberal opinion tonight... [and] decreed a series of laws that put Jews beyond the legal and social pale of the German nation." The newspaper went on to detail the legal import of the new ancestral fractions.

The news was everywhere and inescapable. Centuries of religious prejudice had now been quantified into science. Even if Germans of Jewish ancestry had been practicing Christianity for generations—as many had; henceforth, they would all be legally defined as a race, without regard to their current religion. That was in 1935.

Laughlin's memo to Representative Johnson's House Committee on Immigration and Naturalization regarding Jewish racial quotas eleven years earlier continued to echo: "For this purpose, it would be necessary to define a Jew. Tentatively, such a definition might read, 'A Jew is a person fifty percent or more of whose ancestry are generally recognized as being Jewish in race. The definition applies entirely to race and in no manner to religion.'"

Shortly after the Nuremberg Laws were promulgated in September 1935, and in view of the negative publicity such race laws were receiving, Nazi eugenicist Ernst Rodenwaldt thought it might be helpful to give Laughlin special recognition for his contribution to Reich policy. Rodenwaldt suggested an honorary degree for Laughlin. In a December 1935 letter to Carl Schneider, dean of the University of Heidelberg's medical school, Rodenwaldt wrote, "Every race hygienist knows Laughlin as a champion of eugenic sterilization. Thanks to his indefatigable studies and his indefatigable propaganda activity in America, there exist, since the end of the twenties, in several states of America, sterilization laws and we can report about 15,000 sterilizations until 1930, mainly in California. Professor Laughlin is one of the most important pioneers on the field of racial hygiene. I got to know him in 1927 in Cold Spring Harbor... Heidelberg University honoring professor Laughlin's pioneer work would, in my opinion, make a very good and compensating impression in America, where racial hygienic questions are propagated in the same way as here, but where many questions of the German racial hygienic laws are mistrusted."

Schneider gladly approved the honor. Laughlin could not travel to Heidelberg to accept. But Laughlin expressed his gratitude in a letter to Schneider. "I was greatly honored," Laughlin wrote, "to accept this degree from the University of Heidelberg which stands for the highest ideals of scholarship and research achieved by those racial stocks which have contributed so much to the foundation blood of the American people... I consider the conferring of this high degree upon me not only as a personal honor, but also as evidence of a common understanding of German and American scientists of the nature of eugenics as research in and the practical application of those fundamental biological and social principles."

From 1936 to early 1939, Nazi Germany was considered a threat to the other countries of Europe, and indeed to all humanity. Refugees flooded the world. The Third Reich continued arming for war and demanded territorial concessions from its neighbors. In 1938, the Nazis annexed Austria, and then in early 1939 the Reich overran Czechoslovakia in prewar aggression and consolidation. Concentration camps of gruesome notoriety, from Dachau to Buchenwald, were established across Germany; the horror stories they inspired became common talk of the day. Nazi subversion was a new fear in American society.

Certainly, there were many vocal Nazi sympathizers in America. But those who supported any aspect of the Hitler regime, from economic contacts to scientific exchanges, did so at a substantial moral risk. Genuine revulsion with Nazified eugenics was beginning to sweep over the ranks of previously staunch hereditarians who could no longer identify with a movement so intertwined with the race policies of the Third Reich. A group of longtime eugenicists and geneticists spoke of a profession-wide resolution to disassociate eugenics from issues of race. Letters to Carnegie's Davenport calling for his support were unsuccessful. Institutions such as the Eugenics Research Association, the American Eugenics Society, the Eugenics Record Office and a labyrinth of related entities all remained united in their support of Germany.

Even still, starting about 1936, monthly coverage in *Journal of the American Medical Association* became more skeptical and detached with headlines such as "Strangulation of Intellectualism" placing the Nazi takeover of medical science into clearer perspective. One *JAMA* article unambiguously explained, "The president of the new [medical] society is no distinguished clinician; he is the Nazi district governor of Vienna, that is to say, a politician who is also an official of the Nazi bureau of national health." *JAMA* also began inserting tell-tale quotation marks around Nazi medical expressions and statements to differentiate them from ordinary medical discourse.

After Raymond Fosdick assumed the presidency of the Rockefeller Foundation in 1936, the charitable trust became increasingly unwilling to fund any projects associated with the term *eugenics*, even Fischer's purely genealogical studies. The idea of investigating family trees was just too emblematic of repressive Nazi persecution. Funding was also curtailed for some of the foundation's traditional programs at the Kaiser Wilhelm Institutes. Money continued to flow for eugenic projects, but only when they were cleverly packaged as genetics, brain research, serology or social biology. For example, Rockefeller fellowships and scholarships from 1936 through 1939 allowed German genetic researchers to travel to Cold Spring Harbor and California for further study. But the fact that Rockefeller executives became exceedingly cautious about their continued sponsorship of Nazi medicine was a testament to the controversial nature of any contact with the Third Reich.

Indeed, on June 6, 1939, Fosdick circulated a pointed memo to Rockefeller Foundation executives. "I have read with a good deal of interest your Letter no. 40 of May 25th about our general relation with totalitarian countries, and particularly about the fellowship situation. The rumor which Mr. Kittridge brought back from Geneva to the effect that the Foundation was boycotting all requests from Germany is of course hardly correct... I am frank in saying that at the present moment it would be not only embarrassing, but probably impossible, to make any major grants in Germany. There is a matter of public policy involved here which has to be taken into consideration, and I do not believe that this is the moment to consider any sizable requests for assistance from German sources." Fosdick stipulated that individual fellowships to German scientists would still be possible, but only if "sifted with rigid scrutiny to make sure that we are not being used for ulterior purposes." He added, "I earnestly hope that this evil hour will soon pass."

Despite Nazi Germany's descent into pariah status, core eugenic leaders were steadfast in their defense of, fascination with, and general admiration for Hitler's program. In late 1935, Eugenics Research Association president Clarence Campbell traveled to Berlin for the World Population Congress, an event staged under the patronage of Nazi Interior Minister Frick. Fischer was president of the congress. Campbell created a scandal back home when he loudly and passionately proclaimed his admiration for Hitler's policy. "The leader of the German nation, Adolf Hitler," declared Campbell, "ably supported by Frick and guided by this nation's anthropologists, eugenists and social philosophers, has been able to construct a comprehensive racial policy of population development and improvement that promises to be epochal in racial history. It sets a pattern which other nations and other racial groups must follow if they do not wish to fall behind in their racial quality, in their racial accomplishments and in their prospects for survival."

Campbell's speech made headlines in the next morning's *New York Times*: "US EUGENIST HAILS NAZI RACIAL POLICY." When Campbell returned to America, he struck back at his critics in the lead article of the March–April 1936 issue of *Eugenical News*. "It is unfortunate that the anti-Nazi propaganda with which all countries have been flooded has gone far to obscure the correct understanding and the great importance of the German racial policy."

Throughout 1936, the American eugenic leadership continued its praise for Hitler's anti-Jewish and racial policies. "The last twenty years witnessed two stupendous forward movements, one in our United States, the other in Germany," declared California raceologist C. M. Goethe in his presidential address to the Eugenics Research Association. He added with a degree of satisfaction, "California had led all the world in sterilization operations. Today, even California's quarter century record has, in two years, been outdistanced by Germany."

Eugenicist Marie Kopp toured 15,000 miles across Nazi Germany, and with the assistance of one of the Kaiser Wilhelm Institutes, was able to undertake extensive research on the Nazi program in cities and towns. Kopp was even permitted access to the secret Nazi Heredity Courts. Throughout 1936, Kopp wrote articles for American eugenic publications, participated in promotional roundtables with such luminaries as eugenicist Margaret Sanger, and presented position papers praising the Nazi program as one of "fairness." Kopp was able to assure all that "religious belief does not enter into the matter," because Jews were defined not by their religious practices, but by their bloodlines.

At one American Eugenics Society luncheon, Kopp emphasized, "Justice Holmes, when handling down the decision in the Buck versus Bell case, expressed the guiding spirit... 'It is better for all the world, if instead of waiting to execute degenerate offspring for crime or let them starve for their imbecility, society can prevent those who are manifestly unfit from continuing their kind. Three generations of imbeciles are enough.'"

In 1937, Laughlin and his Cold Spring Harbor office became the U.S. distributor of a two-reel Nazi eugenic propaganda film entitled *Erbkrank* (*The Hereditarily Diseased*). *Erbkrank* began with scenes of squalid German slums where superior Nordic families were forced to live because so much public money was spent on bright, well-constructed institutions to house the feebleminded. Laughlin loaned the film to high schools in New York and New Jersey, to welfare workers in Connecticut, and to the Society for the Prevention of Blindness. Although he acquired the film from the Race Policy Office of the Nazi Party (*Rassenpolitisches Amt der NSDAP*), Laughlin assured, "There is no racial propaganda of any sort in the picture; it is [simply] recognized that every race has its own superior family-stocks and its own degenerate strains."

Yet in fact, the Nazi film declared, "Jewish liberal thinking forced millions of healthy *volk*-nationals into need and squalor—while the unfit were overly coddled." In another frame the movie explained, "The Jewish people has a particularly high percentage of mentally ill." Indeed, one archetypal defective citizen was a mental patient described as a "fifty-five year old Jew—deceitful—rabble-rouser."

No matter how dismal the plight of the Jews in Germany, no matter how horrifying the headlines, no matter how close Europe came to all-out war, no matter how often German troops poured across yet another border, American eugenicists stood fast by their eugenic hero, Adolf Hitler.

After World War II broke out in September of 1939, Carl Schneider helped organize the gassing of thousands of adults adjudged mentally handicapped. The project was codenamed T-4 after the address of the staff, located at Tiergartenstrasse 4 in Berlin. Mass gassings with carbon monoxide, which began in January 1940 at locations across Germany, proved most efficient. Victims were told to undress and to enter a room resembling a shower complete with tiled surfaces, benches and a drain. Crematoria were erected nearby to dispose of the bodies. It was the same Schneider who three years earlier had approved Laughlin's award for the gift of his race science.

At the Nuremberg trials, in their own defense, the Nazis quoted Supreme Court Justice Holmes' words, the California statutes, and the American eugenic principles they brutally emulated. Despite these protestations, the defendants hung.

Returning from a 1935 visit to Germany, the California eugenic leader C. M. Goethe bragged to a key colleague, "You will be interested to know, that your work has played a powerful part in shaping the opinions of the group of intellectuals who are behind Hitler in this epoch-making program. Everywhere I sensed that their opinions have been tremendously stimulated by American thought... I want you, my dear friend, to carry this thought with you for the rest of your life, that you have really jolted into action a great government of 60 million people."

—————————

Sources: Primary documentation for this chapter is drawn exclusively from *War Against the Weak* by Edwin Black.

CHAPTER THREE

Rockefeller, Mengele, and Eugenicide

After the locomotives lurched to a final stop at Auschwitz, after the whistles shrieked and the doors rolled open, after the bewildered masses tumbled out of the boxcars and onto the ramp, above the tumult of their own fear and the incessant barking dogs, all of them heard one word, and they heard it shouted *twice*.

One word shouted twice could help some Jews live even as those next to them were sent to the gas chambers. One word shouted twice would link the crimes of Josef Mengele to a war against the weak waged by the eugenics movement worldwide—from the pastoral shores of Long Island to the reverberating gas chambers of occupied Poland.

As the SS men passed through the trembling crowds lining up for the gas chambers, they cried out for all to hear:

> *Zwillinge! Zwillinge!*
> Twins! Twins!

Lea Lorinczi: *"When we got off the trains, we could hear the Germans yelling, 'Twins, twins!'"* Lea and her brother were spared.

Magda Spiegel: *"SS guards were yelling, 'Twins, twins, we want twins.' I saw a very good-looking man coming toward me. It was Mengele."* They were also spared.

Judith Yagudah: *"When it was our turn, Mengele immediately asked us if we were twins. Ruthie and I looked identical. We had similar hairdos. We were wearing the same outfits. Mengele ordered us to go in a certain direction—and our mother, too."* Judith and Ruthie were spared.

Zvi Klein: *"My twin brother and I were marching toward the gas chambers when we heard people yelling, 'Twins! Twins!' We were yanked out of the lines and brought over to Dr. Mengele."* Zvi and his brother were spared.

Moshe Offer: *"I heard my father cry out to them he had twins. He went over personally to Dr. Mengele and told him, 'I have a pair of twin boys.'… But we didn't want to be separated from our mother, and so the Nazis separated us by force. My father begged Mengele… As we were led away, I saw my father fall to the ground."* The Offer boys lived. Their parents disappeared into the selection.

Why was this word, *"Twins,"* a horrific imperative at Auschwitz? Answer: the Rockefeller Foundation and the odious science it sponsored.

*****

The story centers around Dr. Otmar Freiherr von Verschuer, a hero of the American eugenics movement and a Rockefeller-financed fellow. He would become crucial to the fate of twins at Auschwitz.

Who was Verschuer? Verschuer lived the Nazi ideal before Hitler even emerged. A virulent anti-Semite and a violent German nationalist, he was among the student *Freikorps* militia that staged the Kapp Putsch in March of 1920, preceding the ascent of Hitler. Two years later, Verschuer articulated his eugenic nationalist stance in a student article entitled "Genetics and Race Science as the basis for *Völkische* [People's Nationalist] Politics." "The first and most important task of our internal politics is the population problem…This is a biological problem which can only be solved by biological-political measures."

In 1924, at about the time Hitler staged his Beer Hall Putsch in Munich, Verschuer was lecturing that fighting the Jews was integral to Germany's eugenic battle. He was speaking on race hygiene to a nationalist student training camp when the question of Jewish inferiority came up. "The German, *Völkische* struggle," he told the students, "is primarily directed against the Jews, because alien Jewish penetration is a special threat to the German race." The next year, he helped found the Tübingen branch of Alfred Ploetz's Society for Racial Hygiene and became its secretary. In 1927, Verschuer took a leading role among German race hygienists when he was appointed one of three department heads at the Kaiser Wilhelm Institute for Anthropology, Human Heredity and Eugenics. Verschuer chaired its Human Heredity department.

In 1933, Verschuer published numerous tables setting forth the exact ratios of environmental influences to human heredity. Later that year, when the State Medical Academy in Berlin offered its initial course on genetics and racial hygiene, Verschuer was one of the featured lecturers. He joined other eminent Nazi eugenicists in the program, such as Eugen Fischer and Leonardo Conti, who was a chief Nazi Party health officer and would later become Hitler's main demographic consultant when the 1935 Nuremberg Laws were being formulated. Later, Conti was put in charge of the 1939 euthanasia program.

In June of 1934, Verschuer launched *Der Erbarzt* (*The Genetic Doctor*) as a regular supplement to one of Germany's leading physicians' publications, *Deutsches Ärzteblatt,* published by the German Medical Association. In it, Verschuer asked all physicians to become "genetic doctors," which is why his eugenic publication was a supplement to the German Medical Association's official organ. Sterilization of the unfit was of course a leading topic in *Der Erbarzt*. Eugenic questions from German physicians were answered in a regular "Genetic Advice and Expertise" feature. In the first issue, Verschuer editorialized that *Der Erbarzt* would "forge a link between the ministries of public health, the genetic health courts, and the German medical community." Henceforth, he insisted, doctors must react to their patients not as individuals, but as parts of a racial whole. A new era had arrived, in Verschuer's view: medical treatment was no longer a matter of "doctor and patient," but of "doctor and state."

After the Nazi sterilization law took effect in 1934, German eugenicists were busy creating national card files to cross-index people declared unfit. A plethora of eugenic research institutes were established at various German universities to advance the effort. Their researchers scoured the records of the National Health Service, hospitals and hereditary courts, and then correlated health files on millions of Germans. In this process, Verschuer considered himself nothing less than a eugenic warrior. In 1935, he left the Institute for Anthropology, Human Heredity and Eugenics to found Frankfurt University's impressive new Institute for Hereditary Biology and Racial Hygiene. Boasting more than 60 rooms, including labs, lecture halls, libraries, photography sections, ethnic archives and clinical rooms, the new institute was the largest of its kind in Germany. The institute's mission, according to Verschuer, was to be "responsible for ensuring that the care of genes and race, which Germany is leading worldwide, has such a strong basis that it will withstand any attacks from the outside." More than just a research institute, Verschuer's institution held courses and lectures for the SS, Nazi Party members, public health and welfare officials, as well as medical instructors and doctors, to indoctrinate them with scientific anti-Semitism and eugenic theory.

Soon the Institute for Hereditary Biology and Racial Hygiene had surpassed the Kaiser Wilhelm Institute in race biology and race politics, becoming the new model for German eugenic centers. Verschuer was doing his part to ensure that racial eugenics, the fulcrum of which was rabid Jew-hatred, became the standard for all medical training in Germany. He would soon boast that eugenics had become completely integrated into "the normal course of studies of medical students." In a report to the Nazi Party, he advocated registering all Jews and half-Jews. Hitler, said Verschuer, was "the first statesman to recognize hereditary biology and race hygiene."

By 1937, Verschuer had gained the trust of the highest Nazi

authorities and was beginning to eclipse his colleagues, and by 1939 he was describing his personal role as pivotal to Nazi supremacy. "Our responsibility has thereby become enormous," said Verschuer. "We continue quietly with our research, confident that here also, battles will be fought which will be of greatest consequence for the survival of our people." In an article for a series called *Research into the Jewish Question* (*Forschungen zur Judenfrage*), Verschuer wrote, "We therefore say no to another race mixing with Jews just as we say no to mixing with Negroes and Gypsies, but also Mongolians and people from the South Sea. Our *völkisch* attitude to the biological problem of the Jewish Question... is therefore completely independent of all knowledge of advantages or disadvantages, positive or negative qualities of the Jews... Our position in the race question has its foundation in genetics." In another article he insisted, "The complete racial separation between Germans and Jews is therefore an absolute necessity."

By the early 1930s Verschuer had become a star in American eugenic circles as well, attracting direct and indirect financial support from the Rockefeller Foundation. On May 13, 1932, the Rockefeller Foundation's Paris office had dispatched a radiogram to its New York headquarters asking for $9,000 to further Verschuer's eugenic research while he was at the Institute for Anthropology, Human Heredity and Eugenics.

At the same time, the foundation was already funding an array of vocal German anti-Semites in a five-year $125,000 study. Internal foundation reports described the study as "the racial or biological composition of the German people and of the interaction of biological and social factors in determining the character of the present population." Among the scientists listed on the foundation's roster was Nazi medical murder advocate Ernst Rüdin in project items 9 and 10; and on project item 16 was Verschuer. This $125,000 grant was not made directly, but channeled through the Emergency Fund for German Science (*Notgemeinschaft der Deutschen Wissenschaften*), which evolved into the German Research Society (*Deutsche Forschungsgemeinschaft*).

When Hitler came to power the next year, Rockefeller did not cease its funding of race biology in Germany. However, unlike many American eugenic leaders, Rockefeller officials were more circumspect. Rockefeller executives did not propagandize for Nazism, nor did they approve of the Reich's virulent repression. The foundation's agenda was strictly biological, to the exclusion of politics. It wanted to discover the specific genetic components of the blood of the unfit—even if that meant funding Nazi-controlled institutions.

After attorney Raymond Fosdick assumed the presidency of the Rockefeller Foundation in 1936, the charitable trust became increasingly reluctant to fund any projects associated with the term *eugenics.* Rockefeller money continued to flow into prewar Nazi Germany to fund eugenic projects, but only when the proposals were packaged as "genetics," or "brain research," or "serology" investigations attempting to locate "specific substances" in the blood. However, Rockefeller financing was often too slow for Verschuer, who now sought faster and closer funding through the Reich Research Fund in Berlin, which in the thirties continued to enjoy annual Rockefeller monies. In June of 1939, when the Rockefeller Foundation tried to convince protestors that it was not financing Nazi science, Fosdick was forced to remind his colleagues that such denials were "of course hardly correct." Rockefeller money was still flowing through the Emergency Fund for German Science, now renamed the German Research Society.

Rockefeller's funding of Verschuer was part and parcel of the Nazi's high profile in American eugenics. His career and his writings fascinated the U.S. movement. When Verschuer became secretary of the Tübingen branch of the Society for Race Hygiene in 1925, *Eugenical News* dutifully announced it. His 1926 article on environmental influences for *Archiv für Rassen- und Gesellschaftbiologie* (*Archives of Race Science and Social Biology*) was promptly summarized in *Eugenical News.* The publication also noted Verschuer's 1927 appointment as one of three department heads at the Institute for Anthropology, Human Heredity and Eugenics. In 1928, Verschuer's presence as a guest at an International Federation of Eugenic Organizations meeting was mentioned in *Eugenical News.*

In the years leading up to the ascent of Hitler, his articles continued to be cited in *Eugenical News.*

Even after the Nazis assumed power in 1933, the American eugenic and medical media kept Verschuer in the spotlight. In January of 1934, the *Journal of the American Medical Association* cited a paper he presented at the German Congress of Gynecology. That same month, *Journal of Heredity* reviewed his book on the relationship between eugenics and tuberculosis. In the spring of that year, both *Eugenical News* and *American Journal of Obstetrics and Gynecology* highlighted him as a leader for his work in developing more than a thousand Nazi marriage screening centers. In September of 1934, *JAMA* questioned Verschuer's estimate that the frequency of hereditary blindness in vulnerable populations was a full third, but this only confirmed his status as a major voice in genetic science. That same month, *Eugenical News* published an article entitled "New German Etymology for Eugenics" and cited two definitions for *Rassenhygiene*; Verschuer's definition ran first, and the one by Ploetz—who had invented the discipline—was second. In *Eugenical News*'s next issue, November–December, Verschuer was listed in a feature titled "Names of Eminent Eugenicists in Germany."

By 1935, Verschuer was so admired by American eugenicists that *Eugenical News* heralded the opening of his Institute for Hereditary Biology and Racial Hygiene with the simple headline "Verschuer's Institute." The publication's ecstatic article asserted that Verschuer's new facility was the culmination of decades of preliminary research by Mendel, race theorist Count Gobineau, Ploetz and even Galton himself. Suggesting the far-reaching nature of his enterprise, *Eugenical News* made clear that Verschuer's mission was not merely the "individual man" but "mankind" itself. Among the new institute's several dozen rooms, the paper reported, were a number for "special investigators." *Eugenical News* was so enamored that it departed from its usual text-only format and included two photographs: a picture of the building's exterior plus one of an empty, nondescript corridor. The article closed, "Eugenical News extends best wishes to Dr. O. Freiherr von Verschuer for the success of his work in his new and favorable environment."

Goodwill among American eugenicists toward Verschuer was bountiful. On April 15, 1936, Stanford University anatomist C. H. Danforth wrote to Verschuer offering to translate abstracts of one of Verschuer's journals. On July 7, 1936, Henry Goddard, an architect of America's campaign to use fraudulent intelligence testing to assess eugenic feeblemindedness, sent Verschuer several of his publications hoping that they might be useful to experiments at the new institute. On July 16, 1936, eugenicist Paul Popenoe wrote from the Human Betterment Foundation in California asking for statistics to rebut negative publicity about German sterilizations, saying, "We are always anxious to see that the conditions in Germany are not misunderstood or misrepresented." E.S. Gosney, Popenoe's partner at the Human Betterment Foundation, sent Verschuer three letters and two pamphlets in two months with the latest information on California's sterilization program.

Laughlin himself sent two letters to Verschuer, one in German offering reprints of his own articles and a second in English conveying salutations from America on Germany's accomplishment. Writing on Carnegie Institution ERO letterhead, Laughlin stated, "The Eugenics Record Office and the Eugenics Research Association congratulate the German people on the establishment of their new Institute for the Biology of Heredity and Race Hygiene... We shall be glad indeed to keep in touch with you in the development of eugenics in our respective countries."

Verschuer sent back an effusive letter of appreciation. He congratulated Laughlin on his recent honorary degree from the University of Heidelberg, adding, "You have not only given me pleasure, but have also provided valuable support and stimulus for our work here. I place the greatest value on incorporating the results of all countries into the scientific research that takes place here at my Institute, since this is the only way of furthering the construction of the edifice of science. The friendly interest that you take in our work gives me particular pleasure. May I also be allowed to express my pleasure that you have been awarded an honorary doctorate from the University of Heidelberg and congratulate you on this honor? You have surely concluded from this that we German hereditarians and race hygienists value the pioneering work done by our American colleagues and hope that our joint project will continue to progress in friendly cooperation."

Verschuer and his institute remained prominent in the American medical and eugenic press. When in mid-1935, Verschuer's new institute began deploying a force of young women as field workers to assemble family trees, *Eugenical News* reported it. *JAMA* covered the new institute in-depth in its September 1935 issue, specifying that cards on individuals arising from the investigations were being sent to other Reich health bureaus. *JAMA* reported on Verschuer's work again a few months later in 1936, focusing on his desire to engage in mass research on heredity and illness.

Verschuer's well-received book, *Genetic Pathology* (*Erbpathologie*), claimed that Jews disproportionately suffered from conditions such as diabetes, flat feet, deafness, nervous disorders and blood taint. In its January–February 1936 edition, *Eugenical News* enthusiastically reviewed *Genetic Pathology* and parroted Verschuer's view that a physician now owed his first duty to the "nation," adding, "The word 'nation' no longer means a number of citizens living within certain boundaries, but a biological entity." Verschuer's language on citizenship was a clear precursor to the Reich's soon-to-be-issued decree declaring that Jews could no longer be citizens of Germany, even if they were born there. Stripping German Jews of their citizenship was the next major step toward mass ghettoization, deportation and incarceration. *Eugenical News* closed its review of *Genetic Pathology* with this observation: "Dr. von Verschuer has successfully bridged the gap between medical science and theoretical scientific research."

Verschuer's popularity with American eugenicists had soared by 1937. Senior U.S. eugenicists were clamoring for his attention. Anti-Semite and Nazi sympathizer Charles M. Goethe sent a letter introducing himself. "I am National President of the Eugenics Research Association of the United States," Goethe wrote. "I have heard much of your work at Frankfurt... May I ask whether I could visit your Institution? I feel, because of the violent anti-German propaganda in the United States, our people know almost nothing of what is happening in Germany."

Later that year, Goethe sent an equally fawning correspondence, apologizing for not visiting Germany but appealing to Verschuer's anti-Jewish sentiment. "It was with deep regret that I was unable to come to Frankfurt this year," he wrote. "Dr. Davenport and Dr. Laughlin of the Carnegie Institute have told me so much about your marvelous work... I feel passionately that you are leading all mankind herein. One must exercise herein the greatest tact. America is flooded with anti-German propaganda. It is abundantly financed and originates from a quarter which you know only too well [Jews]... However, this ought to not blind us to the fact that Germany is advancing more rapidly in Erbbiologie than all the rest of mankind."

By 1938, the plight of the Jews in Germany and thousands of refugees had become a world crisis, prompting the Evian Conference. Hitler's Reich had become identified in the media with brutal concentration camps. Germany was again menacing its neighbors' territory. Yet Goethe continued his zealous propagandizing for Nazism. "Again and again," Goethe wrote Verschuer in early 1938, "I am telling our people here, who are only too often poisoned by anti-German propaganda, of the marvelous progress you and your German associates are making." In November of 1938, less than two weeks after the *Kristallnacht* riots, Goethe again wrote Verschuer, this time to lament, "I regret that my fellow countrymen are so blinded by propaganda just at present that they are not reasoning out regarding the very fine work which the splendid eugenists of Germany are doing... I am a loyal American in every way. This does not, however, lessen my respect for the great scientists of Germany."

Clyde Keeler, a Harvard Medical School researcher at eugenic ophthalmologist Lucien Howe's laboratory, visited Verschuer's swastika-bedecked institute at the end of 1938. There he was able to see the center's anti-Jewish program and its devotion to Aryan purity. Upon his return to the United States, Keeler gave fellow eugenicists a glowing report. On February 28, 1939, Danforth of Stanford wrote Verschuer to applaud him, adding that Keeler "thinks that you have by all means the best equipped and most effective establishment of the sort that he has seen anywhere. May I extend my congratulations and express the hope that your group will long continue to put out the same excellent work that has already lent it distinction."

Charles Davenport, who headed up Carnegie's Cold Spring Harbor headquarters, was equally inspired by Verschuer. On December 15, 1937, he asked Verschuer to prepare a special summary of his institute's work for *Eugenical News*, "to keep our readers informed." Davenport also asked Verschuer to join three other prominent Nazi eugenicists on *Eugenical News*'s advisory committee. Falk Ruttke, Eugen Fischer and Ernst Rüdin were already members. With a letter of gratitude, Verschuer agreed to become the fourth. Verschuer was now an essential link between American eugenics and Nazi Germany.

Otmar Freiherr von Verschuer had an assistant. His name was Josef Mengele.

* * * * *

Mengele began his career as a doctrinaire Nazi eugenicist. He attended Rüdin's early lectures and embraced eugenic principles as part of his fanatic Nazism. In 1934 Mengele became a member of the SA, that is, the *Sturm Abteilung*, also known as the Storm Troopers. His first academic mentor was the anti-Semitic eugenicist Theodor Mollison, a professor at Munich University. Just as Goddard claimed he could identify a feebleminded individual by a mere glance, Mollison boasted that he could identify Jewish ancestry by simply examining a person's photograph. Under Mollison, Mengele earned his Ph.D. in 1935. Mengele's dissertation on the facial biometrics of four racial groups—ancient Egyptians, Melanesians and two European types—asserted that specific racial identification was possible through an anthropometric examination of an individual's jawline. Medical certification in hand, Mengele became a practicing doctor in the Leipzig University clinic. But this was only temporary.

Mengele's dream was research, not practice. In 1937, on Mollison's recommendation, Mengele became Verschuer's research assistant at the Institute for Hereditary Biology and Racial Hygiene in Frankfurt. Here Mengele's eugenic knowledge could be applied. Some of Mengele's work involved tracing cranial features through family trees. But Mengele wanted more.

Verschuer and his new assistant quickly bonded. Mengele had applied for Nazi Party membership as soon as the three-year ban on new applicants was lifted in 1937. He and Verschuer made a good professional team. Together the two wrote opinions for the Eugenic Courts enforcing anti-Jewish Nuremberg Laws. In one case, a man suspected of having a Jewish father was prosecuted for engaging in sexual relations with an Aryan woman. Under the Nuremberg Laws, this was a serious criminal offense, calling for prison time. As the prosecution's eugenic consultants, Mengele and Verschuer undertook a detailed examination of the suspect's family tree and carefully measured his facial features. Their eugenic report declared the defendant to be fully of Jewish descent.

However, the accused man provided convincing evidence that he was in fact the illicit offspring of Christians. His father was indeed Jewish, but his mother was not. The man claimed to be the product of his non-Jewish mother's illicit affair with a Christian; hence he was no Jew. Illegitimacy was a common refrain of Jews seeking safe harbor from the Nuremberg statutes. The court believed the man's story and freed him. The decision outraged Mengele and Verschuer, who wrote a letter to the Minister of Justice complaining that their eugenic assessment had been overlooked. Approximately 448 racial opinions were ultimately offered by Verschuer's institute; these were so zealous that Verschuer frequently appealed when the opinions were not accepted.

Mengele's relationship with Verschuer was more than collegial. Staff doctors at the institute recalled that Mengele was Verschuer's "favorite." Verschuer's secretaries enjoyed Mengele's constant visits to the office, and nicknamed him "Papa Mengele." He would drop by the Verschuer home for tea, sometimes bringing his family. Mengele even made an impression on Verschuer's children, who years later remembered him in friendly terms.

In 1938, Mengele joined the SS and received his medical degree, and continued his close association with Verschuer. In fact his SS personnel file, number 317885, listed his employment in 1938 as "an assistant doctor" at the Institute for Hereditary Biology and Racial Hygiene. In the fall of that year, preparing for field assignment with an SS unit, Mengele underwent three months of rigorous basic training. Afterwards, he returned to Verschuer's institute in Frankfurt to resume eugenic research. For example, he examined the inheritance of ear fistulas and chin dimples, and then published the results. In a summary of 1938 projects for the German Research Society, Verschuer listed Mengele's work on inherited deformities and cited two of Mengele's papers, including one he completed for another doctor.

In December of 1938, Mengele and Verschuer, with two other Nazi doctors associated with the institute, requested a grant from the Ministry of Science and Education to attend the International Congress of Genetics in Edinburgh, scheduled for the last week of August 1939. All four men secured initial authorization to attend as part of a large Nazi delegation, approved by the Party. Train and ferry schedules were researched. But after further review, the ministry lacked the funds to send them all. Ministry officials decided Mengele could not go. A few days later, September 1, 1939, Germany began World War II. England and Germany were now enemies, so Nazi conferees returned in the nick of time.

Mengele wanted to get into the war, but a kidney condition prevented him from joining a combat unit. He continued working with Verschuer and in early 1940 was still listed on Institute for Hereditary Biology and Racial Hygiene rosters as being on Verschuer's staff. An internal list of publications and papers, dated January 1939, listed two papers written by Verschuer with the help of assistants including Mengele. One was entitled "Determination of Paternity," recalling their days providing genealogical testimony for the Eugenic Courts. Mengele authored a third paper on the list with two of Verschuer's other assistants.

Mengele also contributed several book reviews to Verschuer's publication, *Der Erbarzt*, in 1940. One review covered a book called *Fundamentals in Genetics and Race Care*, in which Mengele criticized the author for failing to adequately describe "the relationship between the principal races that are to be found in Germany and the cultural achievements of the German people." In another review critiquing a book about congenital heart defects, Mengele complained, "Unfortunately the author did not use subjects where the diagnosis could be verified by an autopsy."

By June of 1940, when Germany was advancing on Western Europe, Mengele could no longer wait to enter the battle. He joined the Waffen SS and was assigned to the Genealogical Section of the SS Race and Settlement Office in occupied Poland. He undoubtedly benefited from Verschuer's March 1940 letter of recommendation averring that Mengele was accomplished, reliable and trustworthy. At the SS Race and Settlement Office, his mission was to seek out Polish candidates for Germanization. He would perform the racial and eugenic examinations. Eventually, in 1941, he was transferred to the Medical Corps of the Waffen SS, and then to the elite Viking unit operating in the Ukraine, where he rendered medical assistance under intense battlefield conditions. Mengele was awarded two Iron Crosses and two combat medic awards. The next year, 1942, as the Final Solution was taking shape, Verschuer arranged for Mengele to transfer back to the SS Race and Settlement Office, this time to its Main Office in Berlin.

By 1942, an aging Fischer was preparing to retire from the Kaiser Wilhelm Institute for Anthropology, Human Heredity and Eugenics in Berlin. His replacement was a major source of debate within eugenic and Nazi Party circles. By this time, Hitler's war against the Jews had escalated from oppressive disenfranchisement to systematic slaughter.

Fischer had emerged as a major advocate of "a total solution to the Jewish question." His view was that "Bolshevist Jews" constituted a dangerous and inferior subspecies. At a key March 1941 conference on the solution to the Jewish problem held in Frankfurt, Fischer had been the honored guest. It was at this meeting that Nazi science extremists set forth ideas on eliminating Jews *en masse*. A leading idea that emerged was the gradual extinction (*Volkstod*) of the Jewish people by systematically concentrating them in large labor camps to be located in Poland. Later, Fischer specified that such labor must be unpaid slave labor lest any "improvement in living standards... lead to an increase in the birth rate."

Given Fischer's high profile in Nazi Party extermination policies, his successor would have to be selected carefully. Lenz was considered for the job, but Fischer worked behind the scenes with the Nazi Party to have Lenz passed over. Fischer thought Lenz was too tutorial, and not bold enough for the challenges ahead. Instead, Fischer's hand-picked successor would be Verschuer—something Fischer had actually planned on for years.

In 1942, Verschuer wrote in *Der Erbarzt* that Germany's war would yield a "total solution to the Jewish problem." He wrote a friend, "Many important events have occurred in my life. I received an invitation, which I accepted, to succeed Eugen Fischer as director of the Dahlem Institute [Kaiser Wilhelm Institute for Anthropology, Human Heredity and Eugenics at Berlin-Dahlem]. Great trust was shown toward me, and all my requests were granted with respect to the importance and authority of the institute... I will take almost all my coworkers with me, first Schade and Grebe, and later Mengele and Fromme." Even though Mengele was still technically attached to the Race and Settlement Office, he was still Verschuer's assistant. Mengele's name even appeared on the special birthday list for the institute's leading staff scientists.

On January 25, 1943, with Hitler's extermination campaign in full swing, Verschuer wrote to Fischer, "My assistant Mengele... has been transferred to work in an office in Berlin [at the SS Race and Settlement Office] so that he can do some work at the Institute on the side."

On May 30, 1943, Mengele arrived at Auschwitz.

* * * * *

Eugenics craved one type of human being above all others to answer its biological questions and to achieve its ultimate biological goal. The quest to locate this type of human being arose at the dawn of eugenics, and continued ceaselessly for four decades, throughout the voluminous discourse, research and publishing of the world-wide eugenic mainstream. To the eugenic scientist, no subject was of greater value. Young or old, healthy or diseased, living or dead, they all wanted one form of human—twins.

Twins were the perfect control group for experimentation. How people developed, how they resisted or succumbed to disease, how they reacted to physical or environmental changes—all these questions could be best answered by twins precisely because they were simultaneous siblings. While fraternal twins sprang from two separate eggs fertilized at the same time, identical twins were, in fact, one egg split in two. Identical twins were essentially Nature's clones.

Twins were valued for a second eugenic reason: Nature itself could be outmaneuvered if desirable individuals could be biologi-cally-enabled to spawn twins—or even better, triplets, quadruplets, and quintuplets. In other words, a world of never-ending multiple births was the best assurance that the planned Aryan super race would remain super.

About a decade before Galton coined the term *eugenics*, he was convinced he could divine the secret of human breeding by study-ing twins. In 1874 and 1875, he published various versions of a scientific essay entitled "The History of Twins as a Criterion of the Relative Powers of Nature and Nurture." In analyzing whether environment or heredity was responsible for an individual's success, Galton complained that his investigations were always hampered by the unending variables—that is, until he located biological compa-rables. "The life history of twins supplies what I wanted," he wrote. Galton had closely studied some 80 sets of twin children by the time he wrote that essay. These included twins of the same and dif-ferent gender as well as identical and non-identical twins.

Cold Spring Harbor's handwritten outlines for key Mendelian traits listed twinning as one of the ten salient physical characteristics to explore. Davenport's 1911 textbook, *Heredity in Relation to Eugenics,* included a section on twins with the introduction, "It is well known that twin production may be an hereditary quality." Three years later, Heinrich Poll, Rockefeller's first fund administrator in Germany, published a major volume on twin research; Poll's interest in the topic dovetailed with the Rockefeller Foundation's years-long support of the subject.

American eugenic publications constantly dotted their pages with the latest twin theory and research. Identifying the mechanism governing the creation and development of twins quickly became a major pursuit for eugenics. In 1916, *Eugenical News* published three articles on the subject, including one that examined a recent article in *Biological Bulletin* on armadillo quadruplets, hoping to apply the principle to multiple births in humans. One of the 1917 articles on twins in *Eugenical News* indicated that in about a quarter of same sex twins, "there is some factor that definitely forces the two children to be of the same sex." A second article in 1917 announced that a doctor in a Michigan institution for the feebleminded was searching the nation for mongolism in twins, especially cases in which only one of the siblings manifested the condition.

The problem with studying twins was that in adulthood most twins lived separate lives, often in separate cities and even in different countries. It was hard to locate them, let alone bring them together for examination. In 1918, the American Genetic Association, the renamed American Breeders Association that helped eugenics get its start, announced that it desired to "communicate with twins living in any part of the world." The AGA explained, "It has been discovered that twins are in a peculiar position to help in the elucidation of certain problems of heredity…'Duplicate' twins have a nearly (though never an absolutely) identical germ plasm… It is fortunate for our knowledge… on account of the chance it gives [us] to study the relative importance of heredity and of environment." Within a year of its announcement, the AGA had identified some 600 twins, and by soliciting photos it had assembled a photo archive of several hundred.

The ERO initiated its own twin study with a detailed four-page questionnaire. Among its numerous questions: "What is your favorite fruit?" and "Do you prefer eggs boiled soft or hard?" It also provided a place for each twin's fingerprints and the names and addresses of family members. ERO investigators located one especially fertile family in Cleveland that had repeatedly produced multiple births. When Davenport wrote up the case for *Journal of Heredity* in 1919, he explained that it had taken more than six visits by field workers to determine the full scope of the original couple's fecundity. Later, *Eugenical News* announced that Columbia, Missouri, was home to more twins than any other city in the nation—one pair for every 477 people.

Hereditarians sought twins of all ages—not just children—for proper study. The family trees of twins fascinated eugenicists, including one New England pair, ninety-one years of age, who garnered much attention in eugenic literature. Geneticists excavated old journals to discover even earlier examples, such as a seventeenth-century Russian woman who gave birth 27 times, each time producing twins, triplets or quadruplets, yielding a total of 69 children.

Race and twins quickly became an issue for American eugenicists. In a 1920 lecture series, Davenport raised the issue of "racial difference in twin frequency" in the same geographic area. He pointed out that from 1896 to 1917, in Washington, D.C., the "negro rate [of twins] is 20 percent higher than the white rate." For whites in the nation's capital, it was 1.82 pairs of twins per hundred births, while blacks had 2.27 per hundred. At about the same time, *Eugenical News,* analyzing recent census data, claimed that twin births overall still occurred at a frequency of approximately 1 percent nationwide; but the percentage of multiple births among Blacks was almost one-fifth greater than among whites. Davenport followed up such observations in his Jamaica race-crossing study, which featured in-depth studies of three sets of twins.

Diagnostic and physiological developments in twin studies from any sector of the medical sciences were of constant interest to eugenic readers. So *Eugenical News* regularly summarized articles from the general medical literature to feed eugenicists' unending fascination with the topic. In 1922, when a state medical journal reported using stethoscopes to monitor a twin pregnancy, it was reported in *Eugenical News*. When a German clinical journal published a study of tumors in twins, this too was reported in *Eugenical News*.

With each passing issue, *Eugenical News* dedicated more and more space to the topic. The list of such reports became long. By the early 1920s, articles on twins became increasingly instructive. One typical article explained how to more precisely verify the presence of identical twins using a capillary microscope. *Journal of Heredity* also made twins a frequent subject in its pages. For example, it published Popenoe's article entitled "Twins Reared Apart," Hermann Muller's article "The Determination of Twin Heredity," and regularly reviewed books about twins.

Every leading eugenic textbook included a section on twins. Popenoe's *Applied Eugenics* explained that identical twins "start lives as halves of the same whole" but "become more unlike if they were brought up apart." Baur-Fischer-Lenz's *Foundation of Human Heredity and Race Hygiene* cited several studies including those written by Popenoe in *Journal of Heredity*. The German eugenicists wrote, "Of late years, the study of twins has been a favorite branch of genetic research" and thanked Galton for his "flash of genius" in "[recognizing] this a long while ago."

In a similar vein, most international eugenic and genetic conferences included presentations or exhibits on twins—their disparity or similarity, their susceptibility to tuberculosis, their likes and dislikes. R. A. Fisher opened one of his lectures to the Second International Congress of Eugenics with the phrase: "The subject of the genesis of human twins... has a special importance for eugenicists." The third congress offered an exhibit on mental disorders in twins, an exhibit illustrating fingerprint comparisons, a third juxtaposing identical and fraternal twins, and a fourth offering an array of 59 anthropometric photos.

The quest for a superior race continued to intersect with the availability of twins. In the July–August 1935 edition of *Eugeni-*

cal News, Dr. Alfred Gordon published a lengthy article entitled "The Problems of Heredity and Eugenics." His first sentence read: "Regulation of reproduction of a superior race (eugenics) is fundamentally based on the principles of heredity." Gordon went on to explain, "The role of heredity finds its strongest corroboration in cases of psychoses in twins." He then gave an example of just two case studies of twins. Such enthusiastic coverage in the biological and eugenic media was prompted a few months before by the extensive examination of just a single pair of twins undertaken at New York University's College of Dentistry, this to identify pathological dentition.

There were so few twins to study that surgeons in the eugenics community passed along their latest discoveries, one by one, to advance the field's common knowledge. In one case, Dr. John Draper of Manhattan wrote to Davenport, "Last Thursday, I opened the abdomen of twin girls, fourteen years old. They presented very similar physical characteristics and the psychoses so far as could be determined were identical." Davenport replied, "Your observations upon the internal anatomy of the twin girls is exceedingly important, as very few observations of this type have been made upon twins." He offered to dispatch a field worker to make facial measurements. Such random reports were precious to eugenicists because physical experimentation on large groups was essentially impossible.

All that changed when Hitler came to power in 1933. Germany surged ahead in its study of twins. The German word for twins is *Zwillinge.* There were tens of thousands of twins in the Reich. In 1921 alone, 19,573 pairs were born, plus 231 sets of triplets. In 1925, 15,741 pairs of twins were born, as well as 161 sets of triplets. Twins were now increasingly sought to help combat hereditary diseases and conditions, real and imagined. Verschuer's book, *Twins and Tuberculosis,* was published in 1933 and received a favorable review in *Journal of Heredity.* In 1934, a Norwegian physician working with Verschuer and Fischer published in a German anthropology journal his analysis of 116 pairs of identical twins and 127 pairs of fraternal twins for their inheritance of an ear characteristic known as Darwin's tubercle.

But many more twins would be needed to accomplish the sweeping research envisioned by the architects of Hitler's master race. In early December of 1935, Verschuer told a correspondent for the *Journal of the American Medical Association* that eugenics had moved into a new phase. Once Mendelian principles of human heredity were established, the correspondent wrote, "Further progress was achieved with the beginning of research on twins, by means of which it is possible to measure hereditary influence even though the hereditary processes are complicated... Many of these researches, however, as Freiherr von Verschuer recently pointed out, are of questionable value... What is absolutely needed is research on series of families and twins selected at random... examined under the same conditions, a fixed minimum of examinations being made in all cases." The article went on to cite Verschuer's view that meaningful research would require entire families—from children to grandparents. In plain words, this meant gathering larger numbers of twins in one place for simultaneous investigation.

To attract more twins, the Nazi Party and the National Socialist Welfare League promoted "twin camps" for the holidays. Verschuer circulated handy text references for all German physicians who might encounter twins. When Verschuer opened his Institute for Hereditary Biology and Racial Hygiene in 1936, the event created such fanfare in *Eugenical News* partially because, "Dr. Verschuer states that the object of his investigation is mankind, not the individual man, but families and twins; and in this work there will not [only] be investigated... interesting twins, but all twins and families of definite geographical origin."

At about that time, German neuropsychiatrist Heinrich Kranz of the University of Breslau published extensive genealogical details about 75 pairs of twin brothers and 50 pairs of opposite gender twins, seeking correlations on criminal behavior. In a *Journal of Heredity* essay, Popenoe lauded Kranz's investigation and predicted that such efforts would help identify "born criminals." Popenoe welcomed more such German research because "it has become one of the most dependable methods of studying human heredity."

Indeed, a plethora of Nazi scientific journals were brimming with regular coverage of eugenic investigations of twins. Several publications were devoted solely to the subject, such as *Zwillings-forschungen* (*Twin Research*) and *Zwillings- und Familienforschungen* (*Twin and Family Research*). Verschuer frequently wrote for these journals. In some cases, Mengele coauthored the articles, including an article on systemic problems and cleft palate deformation published in *Zwillings- und Familienforschungen*. Some published twin research credited Mengele as the principal investigator, such as an article on congenital heart disease, also for *Zwillings- und Familienforschungen*.

Verschuer's preoccupation with twin studies expanded feverishly. He required more and more twins. Rockefeller money was a consistent and conscious supporter of this effort. One of Rockefeller's earliest financial grants for Verschuer's twin research was the $9,000 grant of May 1932 listed as: "KWG Institute [for] Anthropology for research [on] twins and effects on later generations of substances toxic for germ plasm." Other Rockefeller grants for Germany eugenic efforts, such as the Emergency Fund for German Science, repeatedly cited "twins" as a key facet of the research.

Rockefeller's seed money was not wasted. In 1935, *Eugenical News* published a notice entitled "Blood Groups of Twins," which summarized a Nazi medical journal article based on Verschuer's research. "*The Kaiser-Wilhelm Institute für Anthropologie Menschliche Erblehre und Eugenik*, at Dahlem-Berlin," reported *Eugenical News*, "is conducting, through Dr. O. v. Verschuer, studies on twins. Of 202 one-egg twins on whom the blood group was determined, in every case the serologic findings were the same; that is, both fell into the same blood group, just as both are of the same sex. On the other hand, in the case of two-egg twins the blood groups of the twins, whether of same or opposite sex, were frequently unlike."

A cascade of Rockefeller grants to the German Research Society financed Verschuer's continuing heredity research, including a 1935 grant for twin studies. In 1936 and 1937, Verschuer again received funding for twin research and his search for "specific components" in blood.

In a September 1938 application for funds from the German Research Society, Verschuer explained his plans. "Large-scale research on twins is necessary to explore the question of the hereditary aspects of human characteristics, especially illnesses. This research can take two paths: 1. Testing of all twins in a specific geographic area, done at our institute by Miss Liebmann. All twins in the Frankfurt district back to 1898 have been listed and almost all have been examined; she discussed some interesting cases in several articles and a comprehensive summary is being done. 2. Listing of series of twins. Based on cases in over 100 hospitals in west and southwest Germany, the number of twins among them was determined and the cases were examined according to illnesses." He listed rheumatism, stomach ulcers, cancer, heart defects, anemia and leukemia as the conditions he was focusing on. Verschuer assured, "A good deal of material has been collected."

In 1939, Interior Minister Frick issued a public decree compelling all twins to register with their local Public Health Office and make themselves available for genetic testing. The Reich Statistics Bureau would cooperate in the identification campaign. The announcement in the Nazi medical publication *Ziel und Weg* (*Goal and Path*) was published with a lengthy quotation from *Mein Kampf* on the cover: "We must differentiate most stringently between the state as a mere *container* and race as its *contents*. This container is meaningful only when it has the ability to preserve and protect the contents; otherwise it is worthless."

American eugenicist T. U. H. Ellinger was in Germany shortly after the decree to visit with Fischer at the Kaiser Wilhelm Institute for Anthropology, Human Heredity and Eugenics. In a *Journal of Heredity* essay on his visit, Ellinger flippantly reported to his colleagues, "Twins have, of course, for a long time been a favorite material for the study of the relative importance of heredity and environment, of nature and nurture. It does, however, take a dictatorship to oblige some ten thousand pairs of twins, as well as triplets and even quadruplets, to report to a scientific institute at regular intervals for all kinds of recordings and tests."

When twins did report to the Institute for Anthropology, Human Heredity and Eugenics, they were often placed in small, specially-constructed examination rooms, each lined with two-way mirrors and motion picture camera lenses camouflaged into the wallpaper. The staff proudly showed Ellinger all of these facilities. However, eugenicists at the institute could only go so far with mere observations.

Reich scientists needed more if they were to take the next step in creating a super race resistant to disease and capable of transmitting the best traits. Autopsies were required to discover how specific organs and bodily processes reacted to various experiments. Verschuer needed more twins and the freedom to kill them. The highest ranks of the Hitler regime agreed, including Interior Minister Frick, who ran the concentration camps, and SS Chief Heinrich Himmler. Millions of dispensable human beings from across Europe—Jews, Gypsies and other undesirables—were passing through Hitler's camps to be efficiently murdered. Among these millions, there were bound to be thousands of twins.

Shortly after Verschuer took over for Fischer at the Institute for Anthropology, Human Heredity and Eugenics, he proposed a *Zwillingslager*, or "twins camp," within Auschwitz. He applied to the German Research Society, which between July and September of 1943 passed his application through the various steps needed for approval and funding. The grant covered a six-month period beginning in October 1943 under contract number 0296/1595. The camp was approved and was bureaucratically filed under the keyword "Twins Camp."

At the end of May 1943, Mengele arrived in Auschwitz, where he took control of the ramps where Jews were brought in. Verschuer notified the German Research Society, "My assistant, Dr. Josef Mengele (M.D., Ph.D.) joined me in this branch of research. He is presently employed as *Hauptsturmführer* [captain] and camp physician in the Auschwitz concentration camp. Anthropological testing of the most diverse racial groups in this concentration camp are being carried out with permission of the *SS Reichsführer* [Himmler]."

Nazi Germany had now carried eugenics further than any

dared expect. The future of the master race that would thrive in Hitler's Thousand-Year Reich lay in twins. For this reason, there would now be a special class of victims at Auschwitz. There would be a special camp, special medical facilities and laboratories—all for the twins.

After the locomotives lurched to a final stop at Auschwitz, after the whistle shrieked and the doors rolled open, after the bewildered masses tumbled out of the boxcars and onto the ramp, above the tumult of their own fear and the incessant barking dogs, all of them heard one word, and they heard it shouted twice.

As the SS passed through the trembling crowds lining up for the gas chambers, they cried out for all to hear:

> *Zwillinge! Zwillinge!*
> Twins! Twins!

Lea Lorinczi: *"When we got off the trains, we could hear the Germans yelling, 'Twins, twins!'"* Lea and her brother were spared.

Magda Spiegel: *"SS guards were yelling, 'Twins, twins, we want twins.' I saw a very good-looking man coming toward me. It was Mengele."* They were also spared.

Judith Yagudah: *"When it was our turn, Mengele immediately asked us if we were twins. Ruthie and I looked identical. We had similar hairdos. We were wearing the same outfits. Mengele ordered us to go in a certain direction—and our mother, too."* Judith and Ruthie were spared.

Eva Mozes: *"As I clutched my mother's hand, an SS man hurried by shouting, 'Twins! Twins!' He stopped to look at us. Miriam and I looked very much alike. We were wearing similar clothes. 'Are they twins?' he asked my mother. 'Is that good?' she replied. He nodded yes. 'They are twins,' she said."* Eva and Miriam were also pulled out of the gas chamber line.

Zvi Klein: *"My twin brother and I were marching toward the gas chambers when we heard people yelling, 'Twins! Twins!' We were yanked out of the lines and brought over to Dr. Mengele."* Zvi and his brother were spared.

Moshe Offer: *"I heard my father cry out to them he had twins. He went over personally to Dr. Mengele and told him, 'I have a pair of twin boys.'… But we didn't want to be separated from our mother, and so the Nazis separated us by force. My father begged Mengele…As we were led away, I saw my father fall to the ground."* The Offer boys lived. Their parents disappeared into the selection.

Hedvah and Leah Stern: *"Some prisoners told [my mother] in Yiddish, 'Tell them you have twins. There is a Dr. Mengele here who wants twins. Only twins are being kept alive.'"* The Stern sisters lived to tell their story.

All of them lived through the *Selektion*. But now they lived in Mengele's world of torture and testing, electroshock and syringes, eye injections and other hideous experiments—where live children and fresh cadavers were equally prized—all to achieve the eugenic ideal of a superior race in a place where mankind had sunk to the nadir of humanity.

* * * * *

Sadistic science at Auschwitz was part of Nazi Germany's eugenic desire to create its master race.

Like Verschuer, Mengele considered himself a warrior in the battle for eugenic supremacy. In an autobiographical account, Mengele spoke of his desire to create a super race as his initial motive for becoming a doctor. He traced his own family pedigree—pure Aryan stock—back four generations. An inmate anthropologist, Martina Puzyna, saved from death in order to work with Mengele, recalled, "He believed you could create a new super-race as though you were breeding horses… He was mad about genetic engineering." A prisoner pathologist forced to work closely with Mengele wrote that the Angel of Death was obsessed with "the secret of the reproduction of the race. To advance one step in the search to unlock the secret of multiplying the race of superior beings destined to rule was a 'noble goal.' If only it were possible, in the future, to have each German mother bear as many twins as possible."

Shortly after arriving at Auschwitz, Mengele established Verschuer's twin camp at Barrack 14 in Camp F. Mengele had his pick of assistants from the finest doctors and pathologists in Europe, who came to Auschwitz condemned in sealed boxcars. One whom he selected from the ramp was a Hungarian Jewish pathologist named Miklos Nyiszli, a graduate of Friedrich Wilhelm University medical school in Breslau. He became one of Mengele's favorite assistants. Nyiszli's task was to dissect the endless torrent of special corpses and create meticulous postmortem reports. For this process, Mengele would not settle for a typical ramshackle, makeshift concentration camp facility. Instead, amid the filth and squalor of Auschwitz, Mengele requisitioned and created a modern, well-equipped pathology lab.

The lab had everything needed for perfect autopsies. It was eerily professional, with light green painted walls surrounding a red concrete floor. A polished marble dissection table with fluid drains abutted a utility basin with shiny nickel faucets. Three white porcelain sinks lined the wall. Mosquito screens covered the windows. In the adjacent room, Nyiszli found a well-stocked library with the latest publications, three microscopes, and a closet full of mortuary supplies—everything from aprons to gloves. Nyiszli recalled it as "the exact replica of any large city's institute of pathology."

Dina, a Czech inmate known for her skillful paintings, was selected at the ramp to become Mengele's anthropological artist. She would create anatomical drawings of the twins' features: noses, ears, mouths, hands, feet and skulls. Her artwork would accompany the experimentation data in each patient's folder.

Mengele was happy in his work, frequently whistling as he selected human guinea pigs, discarded others to the gas chambers, inflicted his experiments, and then reviewed the autopsies. A broad smile lit up his face as he surveyed his precious subjects, especially the children. "Almost like he had fun," one surviving twin recalled, adding, "He was very playful." Diligent and detailed, he once noticed a smudge on a bright blue file cover and sternly turned to Nyiszli, asking, "How can you be so careless with these files, which I have compiled with so much love!"

Love was a corrupted word for Mengele. He certainly loved his work. At times, he seemed to love the youngest twins. All of Mengele's twins were better fed than other prisoners and even allowed small personal freedoms, such as roaming around the camp. Sometimes he served the children chocolates, patted them on the head affectionately, chaperoned them to camp concerts and made them feel as though he were a father figure looking after them. Eva Kupas remembered that once, when she wanted to see her twin brother, Mengele personally escorted her and "held my hand the whole way." He seemed to identify with one very young boy who somewhat resembled him, and actually trained the child to say "My name is 'Mengele.'"

But without warning, Mengele could fly into uncontrollable murderous frenzies. One teenage girl wept and begged when she was separated from her mother and sisters. She recounted that Mengele "grabbed me by the hair, dragged me on the ground and beat me." When the girl's mother pleaded, Mengele brutally beat her with his riding crop. In one case, a frantic mother fought to remain with her younger daughter. Mengele simply drew his pistol and shot the woman and her daughter, then waved the entire transport to the gas chambers, remarking, "Away with this shit!" Another time he caught a woman named Ibi, who had cleverly evaded the gas chambers six times by jumping off the truck just in time. A suddenly enraged Mengele shrieked, "You want to escape, don't you. You can't escape now! ... Dirty Jew!" As he screamed, Mengele viciously beat the woman to death and kept beating her until her head resembled a bloody, formless mass. After these savage incidents, Mengele could immediately Jekyll-Hyde back to the charming, whistling clinician enchanted with his subjects and his science.

In fact, Mengele loved his twins not because he thought they should be preserved, but only because they briefly served his mad scientific quest. Nyiszli recounted that siblings were subjected "to every medical examination that can be performed on human beings," from blood tests to lumbar punctures. Each was rigorously photographed naked, and callipered from head to toe to complete the record. But these were only the baselines and vital signs. Then came the actual experiments. The Reichenberg boys, mistakenly thought to be twins because they so closely resembled each other, piqued Mengele's interest because one possessed a singer's voice while the other couldn't carry a tune. After crude surgery on both boys' vocal chords, one brother lost his speech altogether. Twin girls were forced to have sex with twin boys to see if twin children would result. Efforts were made to surgically change the gender of other twins.

One day, Mengele brought chocolates and extra clothing for twin brothers, Guido and Nino, both popular with the medical personnel. A few days later, the twins were brought back, their wrists and backs sewn together in a crude parody of conjoined twins, their veins interconnected and their surgical wounds clearly festering. The boys screamed all night until their mother managed to end their agony with a fatal injection of morphine.

Mengele suspected that two Gypsy boys, about seven years of age and well-liked in the lab, carried latent tuberculosis. When prisoner doctors offered a different opinion, Mengele became agitated. He told the assembled staff to wait a while. An hour later he returned and sedately declared, "You are right. There was nothing." After a brief silence, Mengele acknowledged, "Yes, I dissected them." He had shot both in the neck and autopsied them "while they were still warm."

It was imperative that twins be murdered simultaneously to analyze them comparatively. "They had to die together," Nyiszli recounted. For example, the bodies of four sets of Gypsy twins under the age of ten were delivered to Nyiszli for autopsy in one shipment. Twelve sets of gassed twins were diverted from the furnace so they could be dissected as a group; to facilitate identification among the hundreds of twisted corpses, the 12 had been coded with chalk on their chests before they entered the chamber. One girl recovered from an implanted infection too soon; he killed her quickly so both siblings would be freshly deceased.

If, however, one of Mengele's precious human guinea pigs was harmed before he could complete his work, he became incensed.

Guards were under strict instructions to keep Mengele's twins alive, or face his wrath if any died during the night prior to his handling. Some 1,500 twins were subjected to Mengele's atrocities. Fewer than 200 survived. Those who lived had simply not yet been killed.

Mengele also sought dwarfs and the physically deformed—really any specimen of interest. He ghoulishly and capriciously explored the effects of genetics, disease and mass breeding. In one case, Mengele removed part of a man's stomach without administering anesthesia. To investigate the pathology of dysentery, Mengele told Nyiszli to prepare for 150 emaciated corpses, and to autopsy them at the rate of seven per day; Nyiszli protested that he could only complete three per day if he was to be thorough.

Eye color was a favorite subject for experimentation. Eager to discover if brown eyes could be converted to Nordic blue, Mengele would introduce blue dyes, sometimes by drops, sometimes by injection. It often blinded the subjects, but it never changed their eye color.

While evidence of mass murder in the trenches of Russia and the gas chambers of Poland was systematically destroyed, Mengele's murders were enshrined in the protocols of science. Mengele's ghastly files did not remain his private mania, confined to Auschwitz. Every case was meticulously annotated, employing the best scientific method prisoner doctors could muster. Then the files were sent to Verschuer's offices at the Institute for Anthropology, Human Heredity and Eugenics in Berlin-Dahlem for study.

An adult prisoner, chosen to help care for the youngest twins, recounted, "The moment a pair of twins arrived in the barrack, they were asked to complete a detailed questionnaire from the Kaiser-Wilhelm Institute in Berlin. One of my duties as [the] 'Twins' Father' was to help them fill it out, especially the little ones, who couldn't read or write. These forms contained dozens of detailed questions related to a child's background, health, and physical characteristics. They asked for the age, weight, and height of the children, their eye color and the color of their hair. They were promptly mailed to Berlin."

Nyiszli, who had to fill out voluminous postmortem reports, recalled Mengele's warning: "'I want clean copy, because these reports will be forwarded to the Institute of Biological, Racial and Evolutionary Research at Berlin-Dahlem.' Thus I learned that the experiments performed here were checked by the highest medical authorities at one of the most famous scientific institutes in the world."

The reports, countersigned by Mengele and sent to Berlin, were not just received and warehoused, they were carefully reviewed and discussed. A dialogue developed between Verschuer's institute and Mengele. Another prisoner assistant recounted that Mengele "would receive questions about the twins from the Kaiser Wilhelm Institute in Berlin, and he would send them the answers."

The volume of exchange was massive. In a March 1944 memo from Verschuer to the German Research Society, which financed his work, he asked for more clerical assistance and supplies for the Auschwitz project. The memo, entitled "On the continuation of hereditary-psychological research" and filed under the keyword "Twins camp," was coded G for *geheime*, or "secret." Verschuer explained, "Analysis of material obtained from the twins camp continued during the half-year reporting period October 1943 to March 15, 1944. Some 25 psychological analyses, each of which consisted of about 200 pages, were dictated during this period, continuing to round out the overall description of the experiences gained through the twins camp. These analyses were continued, following the same methods as those analyses which began in the summer of 1943. The evaluation system employed has proven useful and was developed further. Several secretaries will be necessary in order to continue the evaluation, as well as sufficient amounts of typing paper, steno blocks and other writing equipment. Some 10,000 sheets of paper will be needed for the coming quarter-year."

More than just reports, Nyiszli sent body parts. "I had to keep any organs of possible scientific interest," he remembered, "so that Dr. Mengele could examine them. Those which might interest the Anthropological Institute at Berlin-Dahlem were preserved in alcohol. These parts were specially packed to be sent through the mails.

Stamped 'War Material—Urgent,' they were given top priority in transit. In the course of my work at the crematorium, I dispatched an impressive number of such packages. I received, in reply, either precise scientific observations or instructions. In order to classify this correspondence I had to set up special files. The directors of the Berlin-Dahlem Institute always warmly thanked Dr. Mengele for this rare and precious material."

Among his many grisly memories, one case especially haunted Nyiszli. Mengele spotted a hunchbacked Jew, a respected cloth merchant from Lodz, Poland, and his teenage son, handsome but with a deformed foot supported by an orthopedic shoe. Mengele ordered his slave pathologist, Nyiszli, to interview the father and son for the file. Nyiszli did so, not in the dissecting room, which reeked of formaldehyde, but in an adjacent study hall, trying his best not to alarm them. After the interview, the father and son were shot. Nyiszli performed detailed autopsies, complete with copious notes. Mengele was fascinated with the eugenic potential of the information, since each individual carried his own deformity. "These bodies must not be cremated," Mengele ordered. "They must be prepared and their skeletons sent to the Anthropological Museum in Berlin." After some discussion, Nyiszli began the gruesome chore of creating two lab-quality skeletons. This involved cooking the corpses to detach all flesh. During the long cooking process in the courtyard, four starving Polish slave workers mistook the contents of the vats and began eating. Nyiszli ran out to stop them. The cooled and treated skeletons were then wrapped in large sacks, labeled "Urgent: National Defense," and mailed to the Institute for Anthropology, Human Heredity and Eugenics.

In the depths of his misery, Nyiszli wondered if he had witnessed too much. "Was it conceivable," he wrote, "that Dr. Mengele, or the Berlin-Dahlem Institute, would ever allow me to leave this place alive?"

Like many eugenic research organizations, the Institute for Anthropology, Human Heredity and Eugenics valued twins for their eyes. For decades, American eugenicists had stressed the research importance of twins' eyes, and the German movement naturally adopted the precept. Indeed, typical enthusiasm for the topic was evident in the March–April 1933 edition of *Eugenical News* in an article headlined "Hereditary Eye Defects," which reviewed a newly released book that included a chapter on "eyes of twins." *Eugenical News* closed its review with the comment, "We have nothing but praise for the assiduity in the gathering of the data... We are happy to have this long needed work done and so well done." Similarly enthusiastic reviews and articles on the subject of twins' eyes and vision were published in *Eugenical News* during the latter 1930s.

In 1936, a colleague had sent Laughlin a request to expand the eye color question of the ERO's Twin Schedule. The new instructions would read: "Look at the colored part of the eye carefully in a good light with the help of a mirror. Is there any difference that you can see in the color or pattern of marks in the right and left eyes? Blue and gray eyes have brownish streaks, sometimes a few, which can be easily counted and usually more in one eye than in the other. Please describe any such difference between your eyes."

Like his American colleagues, Verschuer was long interested in twin eye color. He wanted eye color studies included in his Auschwitz experiments, and the German Research Society funded one such project in September of 1943. Mengele was careful to gather all the eyes Verschuer needed.

Inmate doctor Jancu Vekler never forgot what he saw when he entered one room at the Gypsy camp. "There I saw a wooden table with eyeballs laying on it. All of them were tagged with numbers and little notes. They were pale yellow, pale blue, green and violet." Vera Kriegel, another slave doctor, recalled that she walked into one laboratory and was horrified to see a collection of eyeballs decorating an entire wall, "pinned up like butterflies... I thought I was dead," she said, "and was already living in hell."

One day a prisoner transcriptionist was frantic because while a family of eight had been murdered, only seven pairs of eyes were found in the pathology lab. "You've given me only seven pairs of eyes," the assistant exclaimed. "We are missing two eyes!" He then scavenged similar eyes from other nearby corpses to complete the package for Verschuer's institute—without Mengele being the wiser.

Chief recipient of the eyes was Karin Magnussen, another Verschuer researcher at the institute who was investigating eye anomalies, such as individuals with irises of different colors. In a March 1944 update subheaded "Work on the Human Eye" and submitted to the German Research Society, Magnussen reported, "The first histological work, which was concluded in the fall, 'On the Relationship Between Iris Color, Histological Distribution of Pigment and Pigmentation of the Bulb of the Human Eye,' to be published in the *Zeitschrift für Morphologie und Anthropologie* [*Journal for Morphology and Anthropology*], is currently in press. Material for a second series of experiments is currently being prepared for histological examination. The article on the determination of iris color, which was intended for publication in *Erbarzt* in December 1943, was printed but destroyed by enemy attacks and is now being reprinted. Observations continue on links among certain anomalies in humans. Other observations of humans had to be temporarily suspended for war-related reasons, but are to resume in summer if possible. Material is constantly being collected and evaluated for the expert opinions."

Among the several scholarly articles on eyes from Auschwitz that Magnussen was authoring was one intended for the journal *Zeitschrift für Induktive Abstammungslehre und Vererbungsforschung* (*Journal for Inductive Genealogical Science and Hereditary Research*). Editorial board member Professor George Melchers, who reviewed the submission draft, remembered, "I was struck by the fact that the whole family—grandparents, parents and children—had died at the same time. I could only assume they had [all] been killed in a concentration camp." The war was coming to an end, so Melchers never submitted Magnussen's article to the full board.

Magnussen later told her denazification tribunal, "I became acquainted with Dr. Mengele, who had been inducted as a medical officer, in [Berlin-]Dahlem during the war, when he visited the institute while on leave. I spoke with him a few times during such visits to the institute about scientific projects and scientific problems... I completed my research, although after [a Gypsy] clan with heterochromatic eyes was imprisoned in Auschwitz, I was refused all access to these family members. Completion of my research was only possible through the help given me by Dr. Mengele, who coincidentally had been transferred to the camp. At that time, he helped me trace the hereditary path by determining eye color and family relationships. Through him I also learned that one of the most important families in the clan was contaminated with tuberculosis. I then asked him if he could send me the autopsy and pathological tissue from the eyes if someone from this family should die." She added, "The impression I received from the cases of illness and from the very responsible and very humane and very decent behavior exhibited by Dr. Mengele toward his imprisoned patients and subordinates... was such that I would never have thought that anything could have happened in Auschwitz that violated laws of the state, medicine or of humanity."

In addition to eyes, Verschuer wanted blood. Liters of it. For decades, eugenicists had sought the genetic markers for "carriers," or people who appeared normal but were likely to transmit a Mendelian predisposition for a range of defective traits from pauperism to epilepsy. This effort was at first bogged down in early attempts to assemble race-based family trees and to create pseudoscientific ethnic and class countermeasures. But by the twenties, the most talented eugenicists and geneticists were working hard to analyze blood serum to solve the question of defective germ plasm. They weren't sure whether they were seeking a specific hormone, an enzyme, a protein, genetic material or other blood molecule. They only knew that mankind's eugenic destiny was lurking in the blood and waiting to be discovered.

In 1924, Davenport had told the Second International Congress of Eugenics, "The hormones that determine our personality, constitute the bridge that connects this *personality* on the one hand, with the *specific enzymes* packed away in the chromosomes of the germ cells, on the other." Davenport went on to explain, "You and I differ by virtue of the... atomic activity of the enzymes and hormones which make up that part of the stream of life-yeast which has got into and is activating our protoplasm and will activate that of the fertilized egg that results from us and our consorts." He stressed that a human being was dictated "by virtue of the peculiar properties of those extraordinary activating substances, which are specific for him and other members of his family and race or biotype. The future of human genetics lies largely in a study of these activities... Of these [studies], one of the most significant is that of twin-production."

The *Eugenical News* report on the 1927 grand opening of the Kaiser Wilhelm Institute for Anthropology, Human Heredity and Eugenics, pointed out "In the section on human genetics, twins and the blood groups were specially considered."

German Research Society grants continued through the war years, supporting a broad array of concentration camp experimentation.

In the late summer of 1943, Verschuer received German Research Society funding for serology experiments filed under the keyword "*Spezifische Eiweisskörper,*" alternately translated as "Specific Proteins" or "Specific Albuminous Matter." His project would require voluminous blood samples, as he was seeking the specific blood proteins or albuminous matter that carried genetic traits, from epilepsy to eye color. Verschuer explained in a memo that the blood would come from the Twins Camp at Auschwitz. Mengele, wrote Verschuer, would supervise the operation with the explicit permission of Himmler. "The blood samples are being sent to my laboratory for analysis."

Victim after victim, Mengele extracted large amounts of blood from twins and gypsies. He siphoned it from their arms, sometimes both arms, from the neck, sometimes from fingers. Hedvah and Leah Stern recalled, "We were very frightened of the experiments. They took a lot of blood from us. We fainted several times." One twin survivor remembered years later, "Each woman was given a blood transfusion from another set of twins so Mengele could observe the reaction. We two each received 350 cc of blood from a pair of male twins, which brought on a reaction of severe headache and high fever."

Mengele returned to Berlin from time to time. On one of these trips, he visited his mentor Verschuer for a cozy family dinner. Mengele was asked whether his work at Auschwitz was hard. Years later, Verschuer's son recalled Mengele's reply to his mother: "It's dreadful," Mengele said. "I can't talk about it."

Nevertheless, Mengele was tireless in his bloodletting, his eyeball extractions, his infecting, his autopsying and his selecting, most to the left and some to the right. In mid-August of 1944, his superior filed a letter of commendation. "During his employment as camp physician at the concentration camp Auschwitz," Verschuer asserted, "he has put his knowledge to practical and theoretical use while fighting serious epidemics. With prudence, perseverance and energy, he has carried out all tasks given him, often under very difficult conditions, to the complete satisfaction of his superiors and has shown himself able to cope with every situation."

Years later, Verschuer's medical technician, Irmgard Haase, was interviewed about the work at Auschwitz. She admitted, "There was the research work, which included enzymes in the blood of Gypsy twins and of Russian prisoners of war... From the middle of 1943 onwards, there were several consignments of 30 ml samples of citrated blood." Asked where the blood had come from, she replied, "I don't know. The specimens were in boxes, which had been opened. I never saw the sender's name." She added, "I thought that they were from a camp for prisoners." Auschwitz? "I never heard the word at that time."

Mengele? "Never heard of him." She emphasized, "Specific enzymes in the blood were being investigated by means of... protective enzyme reactions." Were there any misgivings? Haase responded no: "It was science, after all."

* * * * *

Mengele was not alone. Hitler's doctors operated a vast network of laboratories in Nazi concentration camps, euthanasia mills and other places in the territories it occupied. Much of that experimentation was eugenic and genetic, such as the work of Mengele. Much of it was strictly medical, such as the testing at Buchenwald designed to find cures or treatments for well-known diseases. Much of it was simply strategic, such as the cruel ice water and high altitude tests at Dachau intended to benefit *Luftwaffe* pilots bailing out over the North Atlantic.

But even when strictly medical or military testing was inflicted on helpless subjects, it was most often imposed along eugenic lines. More specifically, many Aryans—such as habitual criminals, Jehovah's Witnesses and socialists—were imprisoned in camps under beastly conditions. Mostly, it was the worthless and expendable— Jews, Gypsies, Russians and other "subhuman" prisoners—who were victimized as medical fodder. The exceptions were those Germans considered hereditary misfits, such as homosexuals and the feebleminded. All of it was in furtherance of Hitler's biological revolution and his quest for a master race in a Thousand-Year Reich.

Hitler's master race would be more than just chiseled blond and blue-eyed Nordics. Special breeding facilities were established to mass-produce perfect Aryan babies. They would all be closer to super men and women: taller, stronger and in many ways disease-resistant. Therefore Verschuer was the vanguard of a corps of Nazi medical men who saw the struggle against infirmity and sickness as consonant if not intrinsic to their struggle for eugenic perfection. Nazi Germany was indeed engaged in advanced medical genetics, now amply funded by the Reich's plunder, and militarized and regimented by the fascist state.

Therefore, even as Verschuer and the Kaiser Wilhelm Institute for Anthropology, Human Heredity and Eugenics were supervising the eugenic murders at Auschwitz, they enjoyed military contracts and German Research Society funding to attack a gamut of dreaded inherited diseases. This research could be conducted best in concentration camps such as Buchenwald and Birkenau, or in Kaiser Wilhelm's grandiose complex of centers for higher learning.

For example, Hans Nachtsheim, who also worked under Verschuer, investigated epilepsy and other illnesses under German Research Society aegis and military contract SS 4891-5376, filed under "Research into Heredity Pathology." One typical status memo in October of 1943 reported that, "Experiments on the significance of a lack of oxygen for the triggering of epileptic seizures in epileptic rabbits, which were carried out jointly with Dr. Ruhenstroth-Bauer from the Kaiser Wilhelm Institute for Biochemistry... have essentially been concluded. A preliminary report of the research is currently being printed in the journal *Klinische Wochenschrift* [*Clinical Weekly*]; a comprehensive report is in the process of being drawn up to be published in the journal *Zeitschrift für menschliche Vererbungs- und Konstitutionslehre* [*Journal for Science of Human Genetics and Constitution*]."

The depth of Nachtsheim's learning was evident. "Further experiments," he continued, "are concerned with the effect of the epilepsy gene in association with other genes [*Gengesellschaft*]. It has been determined that a single dosage of the epilepsy gene may suffice to induce epilepsy in combination with certain other genes, although the epilepsy gene is usually recessive, meaning that it must be present in a double dosage in order to become effective. Thus, a carrier of two albino genes and a single epilepsy gene can become an epileptic. The albino gene is the most extreme and most recessive allele [chromosomal pair] of a series of 6 alleles. In order to understand the essence of genes and their interaction, it is important to know how the other alleles act in combination with the epilepsy gene. Up to now, it could be proven that the allele most closely related to the albino gene...reacts just as the albino factor, while the normal allele, which is dominant over all other alleles in the series, suppresses the outbreak of epilepsy even in a single dosage in the presence of even one epilepsy gene. Experiments with the other alleles remain to be done."

Verschuer studied tuberculosis in rabbits under German Research Society aegis and contract SS 4891-5377. One typical report explained that, "In addition to crossbreeding, pure breeding continued; in particular, the attempt was made to determine why the members of one family were always killed by lung tuberculosis while this form did not develop in the other family. The attempt was made to change the way in which tuberculosis presented in the various breeds. This was done by means of sac blockage, reinfections and organ implants. These experiments have not yet been concluded, but it appears that the development of tuberculosis in the breeds is extremely resistant. It will be necessary to expand these experiments, since their results could be of fundamental significance for the treatment of tuberculosis in humans."

Similar genuine science could be seen in the other reports of the various Kaiser Wilhelm Institutes. One of them was the Institute for Brain Research, an organization financed by Rockefeller money from the ground up starting in the late 1920s. Senior researchers Drs. Julius Hallervorden and Hugo Spatz published their pioneering work on a form of inherited brain degeneration, which was eventually named Hallervorden-Spatz Syndrome. After Institute for Brain Research founder Oskar Vogt was removed for his lack of Nazi activism, Spatz took his place and the organization was fully integrated into the Nazi killing process. While Hallervorden held the neuropathology chair at the Institute for Brain Research, he was also appointed senior physician at Brandenburg State Hospital, one of six institutions operating gas chambers under the T-4 euthanasia program. Ultimately, more than 70,200 Germans classed feebleminded were gassed under T-4. In 1938, four autopsies were performed at the Brandenburg facility. During the next five years, 1,260 would be completed. The brains—nearly 700—went to Hallervorden.

Hallervorden to his interrogators after the war: "I heard that they were going to do that, and so I went up to them and told them, 'Look here now, boys, if you are going to kill all those people, at least take the brains out so that the material could be utilized.' ... There was wonderful material among those brains, beautiful mental defectives, malformations and early infantile disease... They asked me: 'How many can you examine?' and so I told them an unlimited number—the more the better... They came bringing them in like the delivery van from the furniture company. The Public Ambu-

lance Society brought the brains in batches of 150-250 at a time...
I accepted the brains, of course."

Direct Rockefeller funding for Hallervorden and Spatz's Institute for Brain Research during the Hitler regime stopped in 1934, and funding for Rüdin's Kaiser Wilhelm Institute for Psychiatry ended in 1935. However, there were undoubtedly additional Rockefeller funds made available to institute researchers through the German Research Society. Rockefeller also provided the seed money for research at the Kaiser Wilhelm Institute for Biology until the war broke out in 1939. Moreover, the Foundation continued to fund individual physicians, such as Tübingen forensic psychiatrist Robert Gaupp, Breslau patho-psychologist Kurt Beringer, Munich psychiatrist Oswald Bumke and Freiburg neurologist Werner Wagner, each affiliated with his own institution. During these years, Rockefeller also subsidized social scientists in Nazi-annexed Vienna. Much of this money continued until 1939. During the thirties, millions in Rockefeller Foundation grants also flowed to other Kaiser Wilhelm Institutes devoted to the physical sciences. One such was the Kaiser Wilhelm Institute for Physical Chemistry and Electrochemistry, which was engaged in weapons research.

The mentality behind the foundation's biological funding could best be seen in the words of Rockefeller Natural Science Director Warren Weaver. Just a few months after Hitler came to power in 1933, Weaver circulated a report to the trustees entitled "Natural Sciences—Program and Policy: Past Program and Proposed Future Program." That report asserted, "Work in human genetics should receive special consideration as rapidly as sound possibilities present themselves. The attack planned, however, is a basic and long-range one." A year later, Weaver asked "whether we can develop so sound and extensive a genetics that we can hope to breed, in the future, superior men?"

In pursuing its breeding goals, the Rockefeller Foundation could reassure itself and others that it was not actually furthering the increasingly discredited pseudoscience of eugenics. In fact, that 1933 report to the trustees specifically stated, "The attack [for heredity research] planned, however, is a basic and long-range one, and such a subject as eugenics, for example, would not be given support." After rejecting eugenics by name, the report went on to advocate that "support should be continued and extended to include the biochemical, physiological, neurological and psychological aspects of internal secretions in general."

But while openly eschewing eugenics with statements and memos, Rockefeller in fact turned to eugenicists and race scientists throughout the biological sciences to achieve the same goal creating a superior race.

Rockefeller never knew of Mengele. With few exceptions, the foundation had ceased all eugenic studies in Nazi-occupied Europe when the war erupted in 1939. But by that time the die had been cast. The talented men Rockefeller financed, the great institutions it helped found, and the science it helped create had taken on a scientific momentum of their own.

What could have stopped the race biologists of Berlin, Munich, Buchenwald and Auschwitz? Certainly, the Nazis felt they were unstoppable. They imagined a Thousand-Year Reich of super-bred men. Hence when the twins, the prisoner doctors and those selected for the gas chamber looked at Mengele, time after time they reported the piercing look in his eyes. That look—Mengele's glare—was the Nazi vision wedded to a fanatical science whose soul had been emptied, its moral compass cracked; a science backed not merely by iron dogma but by men wielding machine guns and pellets of *Zyklon B*. All of them were versed in the polysyllabics of cold clinical murder. Surely, to the victims of Auschwitz, it must have seemed like nothing could stop Nazi science from its global biological triumph.

But something did defeat Mengele and his colleagues. Not reason. Not remorse. Not sudden realization. Nazi eugenicists were impervious to those powers. But two things did stop the movement. On June 6, 1944, the Allies invaded at Normandy and began defeating the Nazis, town by town and often street by street. They closed in on Germany from the west. The Russian army overran the Auschwitz death camp from the east on January 27, 1945. Mengele fled.

Hence, Auschwitz was indeed the last stand of American-inspired eugenics. The science of the strong almost completely prevailed in its war against the weak. Almost.

Sources: Primary documentation for this chapter is drawn exclusively from *War Against the Weak* by Edwin Black.

CHAPTER FOUR

GM and the Motorization of the Reich

Suddenly the dull camouflage beige-brown and green Blitz trucks rolled into the village not far from the Polish border. Commanders rode ahead and behind in military cars. Moments later, troops jumped from the back and took up positions throughout the village. Soon the Jews would be herded, dragged, and pulled onto those trucks to be transported to their destiny with the Nazi war machine. Some were destined for bitter labor. Some were destined for a bitter ghetto. For too many, their destiny was a terrible extermination.

Germany's onslaught was dazzling in its deadliness. Nazi war vehicles were powerful, well-built machines. With those trucks, the Nazis could roll and resupply anywhere in Europe as they waged *blitzkrieg*, or lightning war. The motorized *blitzkrieg* began at 6 AM September 1, 1939 when WWII broke and never stopped until the last gasp of surrender in early May 1945. Using trucks and command cars, the Third Reich conquered, occupied and decimated Europe.

In every country, the Jews were singled out first and with precision. Indeed, Germany's murderous blitz against the Jews was waged with the type of efficiency that only a motorized murder machine could inflict. In every city neighborhood, every small town, and every remote village, the Germans could deploy a swift, mobile, and unstoppable campaign.

The Germans had been able to achieve something no other anti-Jewish measure could accomplish. Earlier campaigns to suppress Jews had been limited to men on horseback, moving slowly just 5 to 15 mph. Indeed, 20 years earlier, WWI itself had been waged principally on horseback. This time it was different. This time they came in trucks and cars, and wreaking their havoc at high-speed.

It all came about so rapidly—in just nine years. When Hitler came to power, a Germany wracked by the Depression lacked the mass production, oil and roads to function as a nation on wheels. Within just six years, Hitler transformed his horse-and-wagon nation into an automotive power complete with a newly constructed Autobahn. How did Germany make the monumental transition from a horse-drawn army to a motorized murder machine capable of waging *blitzkrieg*? Answer: General Motors, the Reich's dependable chief truck and car manufacturer. Indeed, the company made the three-ton Blitz truck precisely for the *Blitzkrieg*.

General Motors and Opel were eager, willing and indispensable cogs in the Third Reich's rearmament juggernaut, a rearmament that, as many feared during the 1930s, would enable Hitler to conquer Europe and destroy millions of lives. GM and its president, Alfred P. Sloan, worked continuously for years to mobilize the Third Reich. They cooperated with virtually every aspect of Hitler's Nazi revolution and economic recovery plan. At the same time, the company undermined the New Deal of Franklin D. Roosevelt by systematically subverting America's electric mass transit, making it dependent upon oil. This oil dependency came at a time when war planners nervously counted every Axis and Allied barrel of petroleum as the difference between victory and defeat.

The Detroit-Berlin axis began early on, and at the top.

* * * * *

James D. Mooney thrust his arm diagonally, watching its reflection in his hotel suite mirror. Not quite right. He tried once again. Still not right. Was it too stiff? Too slanted? Should his palm stretch perpendicular to the ceiling; should his arm bend at a severe angle? Or should the entire limb extend straight from shoulder to fingertips? Should his *Sieg Heil* project enthusiasm or declare obedience? Never mind, it was afternoon. Time to see Hitler.

Just the day before, May 1, 1934, under a brilliant, cloudless sky, Mooney, President of the General Motors Overseas Corporation, climbed into his automobile and drove toward Tempelhof Field at the outskirts of Berlin to attend yet another hypnotic Nazi extravaganza. This one was the annual "May Day" festival.

Tempelhof Field was a sprawling, oblong-shaped airfield. But for May Day, the immense site was converted into parade grounds. Security was more than tense, it was paranoid. All cars entering the area were meticulously inspected for anti-Hitler pamphlets or other contraband. But not Mooney's. *Der Führer's* office had sent over a special windshield tag that granted the General Motors' chief *carte blanche* to any area of Tempelhof. Mooney would be Hitler's special guest.

As Mooney arrived at the airfield, about 3:30 in the afternoon, the spectacle dazzled him. Sweeping swastika banners stretching 33 feet wide and soaring 150 feet into the air fluttered from 43-ton steel towers. Each tower was anchored in 13 feet of concrete to resist the winds as steadfastly as the Third Reich resisted all efforts to moderate its program of rearmament and oppression.

Thousands of other Nazi flags fluttered across the grounds as dense column after column of Nazis, marching shoulder to shoulder in syncopation, flowed into rigid formation. Each of the 13 parade columns boasted between 30,000 and 90,000 storm troopers, army divisions, citizen brigades and blond haired, blue-eyed Hitler Youth enrollees. Finally, after four hours, the tightly packed assemblage totaled about 2 million marchers and attendees.

Hitler eventually arrived in an open-air automobile that cruised up and down the field amid the sea of devotees. Accompanied by cadres of SS guards, Hitler was ushered to the stage, stopping first to pat the head of a smiling boy. This would be yet another grandiose spectacle of *Führer*-worship so emblematic of the Nazi regime.

When ready, Hitler launched into one of his enthralling speeches, made all the more mesmerizing by 142 loudspeakers sprinkled throughout the grounds. As *der Führer* demanded hard work and discipline, and enunciated his vision of National Socialist destiny, the crisp sound of his voice traveled across an audience so vast that it took a moment or two for his words to reach the outer perimeter of the throng. Hence, the thunderous applause that greeted Hitler's remarks arrived sequentially, creating an aural effect of continuous, overlapping waves of adulation.

General Motors World, the company house organ, covered the May Day event glowingly in a several-page cover story, stressing Hitler's boundless affinity for children. "By nine, the streets were full of people waiting to see Herr Hitler go meet the children," the publication reported.

The next day, May 2, 1934, after practicing his *Sieg Heil* in front of a mirror, Mooney and two other senior executives from General Motors and its German division, Adam Opel A.G., went to meet Hitler in his Chancellery office. Waiting with Hitler would be Nazi Party stalwart Joachim von Ribbentrop, who would later become foreign minister, and Reich economic adviser Wilhelm Keppler.

As Mooney traversed the long approach to Hitler's desk, he began to pump his arm in a stern-faced *Sieg Heil*. But *der Führer* surprised him by getting up from his desk and meeting Mooney halfway, not with a salute but a businesslike handshake. This was, after all, a meeting about business.

Hitler knew that the biggest auto and truck manufacturer in Germany was not Daimler or any other German carmaker. The biggest automotive manufacturer in Germany—indeed in all of Europe—was General Motors. Since 1929, GM had owned and operated the long-time German firm Opel. GM's Opel, infused with millions in GM cash and assembly-line know-how, produced some 40 percent of the vehicles in Germany and about 65 percent of its exports. Indeed, Opel dominated Germany's auto industry.

Beyond impressive production statistics, *der Führer* was simply fascinated with every aspect of the automobile, its history, its inherent liberating appeal and, of course, its application as a weapon of war. German automotive engineers were famous for their engineering innovations. But the lack of ready petroleum supplies and gas stations in Germany, coupled with the nation's massive depression unemployment, kept autos out of reach for the common man in Nazi Germany. In 1928, just before the Depression hit, one in five Americans owned a car, while in Germany, ownership was one in 134.

In fact, just two months before Mooney's meeting at the Chancellery, Hitler had commented at the Berlin International Automobile and Motor Cycle Show: "It can only be said with profound sadness that, in the present age of civilization, the ordinary hardworking citizen is still unable to afford a car, a means of up-to-date transport and a source of enjoyment in the leisure hours."

Even if few Germans could afford cars—those made by GM or otherwise—the company did provide many in the Third Reich with jobs. Hitler was keenly aware that GM, unlike German carmakers, used mass production techniques pioneered in Detroit, so-called "Fordism" or "American production."

As the May 2, 1934 Chancellery meeting progressed, Hitler thanked Mooney and GM for being a major employer—some 17,000 jobs—in a Germany where Nazi success hinged on re-employment. Moreover, since Opel was responsible for some 65 percent of auto exports, the company also earned the foreign currency the Reich desperately needed to purchase raw materials for re-employment as well as for the regime's crash rearmament program. Now, as Hitler embarked on a massive, threatening re-armament program, GM was in a position to make Germany's military a powerful, modern, and motorized marvel.

During the meeting with Mooney, Hitler estimated that if Germany were to emulate American ratios, the Reich should possess some 12 million cars. But, Hitler added, only three million cars was a more realistic target under the circumstances. Even this, he assured, would be a vast improvement over the 104,000 vehicles manufactured in Germany in 1932.

Mooney was enthusiastic. He told Hitler that GM was willing to mass produce a cheap car, costing just 1,400 marks, with the mass appeal of Henry Ford's Model T, if the Nazi regime could guarantee 100,000 car sales annually, issue a decree limiting dealer commissions and control the price of raw materials. Many automotive concerns were vying for the chance to build Hitler's dream, a people's car or a so-called "*volkswagen*." But GM was convinced that it alone possessed the proven production know-how. An intrigued Hitler showering his GM guests with questions.

Would the cost of garaging a car be prohibitive for the average man? Could vehicles parked outdoors be damaged by the elements? Mooney answered that the same vehicle built to withstand wind, dust and rain at 40 mph to 60 mph could stand up to overnight exposure outdoors. To promote automobile ownership, Hitler even promised something as trivial as legalized street parking.

Hitler had previously committed the Reich to expedite completion of the world's first transnational network of auto highways, the Autobahn. Now, to further promote motorcar proliferation, Hitler suggested to Mooney that the German government could also reduce gasoline prices and gasoline taxes. Hitler even asked if Opel could advise him how to prudently reduce car insurance rates, thus lowering overall operating costs for average Germans.

The conference in Hitler's Chancellery office, originally scheduled for a quarter hour, stretched to 90 minutes.

The next morning, May 3, 1934, an excited Hitler told Keppler, "I have been thinking all night about the many things that these Opel men told me." He instructed Keppler, "Get in touch with them before they leave Berlin." Hitler wanted to know still more. Later that day, Mooney spent hours ensconced in his hotel suite composing written answers to *der Führer's* many additional questions.

Clearly, Hitler saw the mass adoption of autos as part of Germany's great destiny. No wonder Mooney and GM were optimistic about the prospects for a strategic relationship with Nazi Germany.

A few weeks after the prolonged Chancellery session, the company publication, *General Motors World*, effusively recounted the meeting, proclaiming, "Hitler is a strong man, well fitted to lead the German people out of their former economic distress... He is leading them, not by force or fear, but by intelligent planning and execution of fundamentally sound principles of government."

Ironically, Hitler's famous inability to follow up on ideas caused GM officials to wonder if they had been too revealing in their company publication's coverage of the Chancellery meeting. Indeed, copies of *General Motors World* were seized by Opel company officials before they could circulate in Germany. Mooney later declared he would do nothing to make Adolf Hitler angry.

For Mooney and for GM's German branch, the relationship with the Third Reich was first and foremost about making money —billions in 21st century dollars—off the Nazi desire to re-arm.

Significantly, the commanding, decision-making force at the carmaker was not Mooney, GM's man in Nazi Germany. Rather, it was the company's cold and calculating chief executive, the man who operated out of corporate headquarters in Detroit and New York to orchestrate the firm's involvement with the Third Reich. It was GM president Alfred P. Sloan.

Who was Sloan?

It would be easy to call Sloan "Mr. Big." Sloan lived for bigness. Slender and natty, attired in the latest collars and ties, Sloan commonly wore spats, even to the White House. He often out-dressed his former GM boss, billionaire Pierre du Pont. An electrical engineer by training, the Massachusetts Institute of Technology graduate was a shrewd, strategic thinker driven by a compulsion to grow his company as much he was compelled to breathe oxygen. He said as much. "Deliberately to stop growing is to suffocate," Sloan wrote about his years at GM, adding, "We do things in a big way in the United States. I have always believed in planning big, and I have always discovered after the fact that, if anything, we didn't plan big enough. I put no ceiling on progress."

For Sloan, motorizing the fascist regime that was expected to wage a bloody war in Europe was the "next big thing" and a spigot of limitless profits for GM. But unlike many commercial collaborators with the Nazis who were driven strictly by the icy quest for profits, Sloan also harbored a political motivation. Sloan despised the emerging American way of life being crafted by President Franklin Delano Roosevelt. Sloan hated Roosevelt's New Deal, and admired the strength, irrepressible determination and sheer magnitude of Hitler's vision.

For Sloan, the New Deal—with its Social Security program, government regulation and support for labor unions—clanged an unmistakable death knell for an America made great by great corporations guided by great corporate leaders.

In a 1934 letter to Roosevelt's Industrial Advisory Board, Sloan complained bitterly that the New Deal was attempting to change the rules of business so "government and not industry [shall] constitute the final authority." In Sloan's view, GM was bigger than mere governments, and its corporate executives were vastly more suited to decision-making than "politicians" and bureaucrats who he felt were profoundly unqualified to run the country. Government officials, Sloan believed, merely catered to voters and prospered from backroom deals.

Sloan's disdain for the American government went beyond ordinary political dissent. The GM chief so hated the President and his administration that he co-founded a virulently anti-Roosevelt organization and donated to at least one other Roosevelt-bashing group. Moreover, Sloan actually pressured GM executives not to serve in government positions, although many disregarded his advice and loyally joined the government's push for war preparedness.

At one point, Sloan's senior officials at GM even threatened to launch a deliberate business slowdown to sabotage the administration's recovery plan. At the same time, Sloan and GM did not fail to express admiration for the stellar accomplishments of the Third Reich, and went the extra mile to advance German economic growth.

Indeed, Sloan felt that GM could—and should—create its own foreign policy and back the Hitler regime even as America recoiled from it. "Industry must assume the role of enlightened industrial statesmanship," Sloan declared in an April 1936 quarterly report to GM stockholders. "It can no longer confine its responsibilities to the mere physical production and distribution of goods and services. It must aggressively move forward and attune its thinking and its policies toward advancing the interest of the community at large, from which it receives a most valuable franchise."

In ramping up auto production in the Nazi Reich, Sloan understood completely that he was not just manufacturing vehicles. Sloan and Hitler both knew that GM, by creating wealth and shrinking unemployment, was helping to prop up the Hitler regime.

When explaining his ideas of mass production to Opel car dealers, Sloan proudly declared what the enterprise would mean: "The motor car contributes more to the wealth of the United States than agriculture. The automobile industry is a wealth-creating industry." What was true in America would become true in Germany. Ironically, GM chose the alliance with Hitler even though doing so threatened to imperil GM at home. Just days after Hitler came to power on January 30, 1933, a worldwide anti-Nazi boycott erupted, led by the American Jewish Congress, the Jewish War Veterans and a coalition of anti-fascist, pro-labor, interfaith and American patriotic groups. Their objective was to fatally fracture the German economy, not resurrect it.

The anti-Nazi protesters vowed not only to boycott German goods, but to picket and cross-boycott any American companies doing business with Germany. In the beginning, few understood that in boycotting Opel of Germany, they were actually boycotting GM of Detroit. Effectively, they were one and the same.

GM's determination to re-arm Germany intensified even as the world expected that Germany would plunge Europe and America into a devastating war.

Typical of news coverage of events at the time was an article in the March 26, 1933, edition of *The New York Times*, headlined "Hitler a Menace." The article, quoting former Princeton University President John Hibben, echoed the war fear spreading across both sides of the Atlantic. "Adolf Hitler is a menace to the world's peace, and if his policies bring war to Europe, the United States cannot escape participating," the article opened. This was just one of dozens of such articles that ran in American newspapers of the day, complemented by continuous radio and newsreel coverage warning that Germany would lead the world back to war.

Beyond the Reich determination to go back to war, Sloan also knew that terrible anti-Jewish persecution was underway in Germany. Indeed, by the spring of 1933, the entire world was beginning to learn about the lawlessness and anti-Semitic savagery of the Nazi regime.

On March 27, 1933, a million protesters jammed Madison Square Garden in New York, and millions more around the world joined in a coordinated show of protest against Nazi brutality. By May 10, 1933, Nazi-banned books were being torched in public bonfires across Germany. The front page stories and newsreels were continuous. In fact, the corporate library at General Motors' Opel in Germany was also purged of Jewish-authored publications and other undesirable literature.

Beginning in the late spring of 1933, concentration camps such as Dachau were generating headlines reporting unspeakable brutality.

By June 1933, Jews everywhere in Germany were being banned from the professional, economic and cultural life of the country. As state-designated pariahs, they were forbidden to remain members of the German Automobile Association, the popular organization for the general German motorist. Hitler's anti-Semitic demagoguery and the daily, semi-official, violent attacks against Jews were discussed in the American media almost daily.

Nonetheless, GM and Germany embarked full-speed upon their strategic business relationship. That relationship was hardly one focused on passenger vehicles for average Germans.

Quickly, Sloan and James D. Mooney, GM's overseas chief, realized that the Reich military machine was in fact the corporation's best customer in Germany. Sales to the army yielded a greater per truck profit than civilian sales—a hefty 40 percent more. So GM preferred supplying the *Wehrmacht,* the German military, which never ceased its preparations to wage war against Europe.

In 1935, GM agreed to locate a new factory at Brandenburg,

where it would be geographically less vulnerable to feared aerial bombardment by allied forces. In 1937, almost 17 percent of Opel's Blitz trucks were sold directly to the Nazi military.

That military sales figure was increased to 29 percent in 1938 —totaling some 6,000 Blitz trucks that year alone. The *Wehrmacht* soon became Opel's No. 1 customer by far. The Blitz became the mainstay of the German army. Other important customers included the major industries associated with the Hitler war machine.

Expanding its German workforce from 17,000 in 1934 to 27,000 in 1938 also made GM one of Germany's leading employers. Unquestionably, GM's Opel became an integral facet of Hitler's Reich.

More than just an efficient manufacturer, Opel openly embraced the bizarre philosophy that powered the Nazi military-industrial complex. The German company participated in cultic *Führer* worship as a part of its daily corporate ethic. After all, until GM purchased Opel in 1929 for $33.3 million, or about one-third of GM's after-tax profit that year, Opel was an established carmaker with a respected German persona. The Opel family included several prominent Nazi Party members. This identity appealed to rank-and-file Nazis who condemned anything foreign-owned or foreign-made. For all these reasons, during the Hitler years, Sloan and Mooney both made efforts to obscure Opel's American ownership and control.

As a result, the average storm trooper, Nazi Party member or German motorist accepted the company's cars and trucks as the product of a purely Aryan firm that was working toward Hitler's great destiny: "*Deutschland uber alles.*"

As a loyal Nazi entity, Opel did all the right things. Opel became an early patron of the National Socialist Motor Corps, a rabid Nazi Party paramilitary auxiliary. Ironically, most of the members of Corps were not drivers, but Germans seeking to learn how to drive to increase national readiness. Opel employees were encouraged to maintain membership in the Motor Corps. Furthermore, Opel cars and trucks were loaned without charge to the local storm trooper contingents stationed near company headquarters at Russelsheim,

Germany. As Brownshirt thugs went about their business of intimidation and extortion, they often came and went in vehicles bearing prominent Opel advertisements, proud automobile sponsor of the storm troopers.

The Opel company publication, *Der Opel Geist*, or *The Opel Spirit*, became just another propagandistic tool of Führer worship, edited with the help of Nazi officials. Hitler was frequently given credit in the publication for Opel's achievements, and was frequently depicted in *Der Opel Geist* portraits and illustrations as a fatherly or stately figure.

It was not just *der Führer's* image. Hitler's voice regularly echoed through the cavernous Opel complex. His hate speeches and pep rallies were routinely piped into the factory premises to inspire the workers. Great swastika-bedecked company events were commonplace, as Nazi *gauleiters*, that is regional party leaders, and other NSDAP officials spurred gathered employees to work hard for *der Führer* and his Thousand-Year Reich. Opel contributed large cash donations to all the right Nazi Party activities. For example, the company gave local storm troopers 75,000 reichsmarks to construct the local *gauleiter's* new office headquarters.

In the process, Opel became more than a mere carmaker. It became a stalwart of the Nazi community. Working hard and meeting exhausting production quotas were national duties. Employees who protested the intense working conditions, even if they were members of the Nazi Party, were sometimes visited by the Gestapo. SS officers worked as internal security throughout the plant. Order was kept. Production quotas were met.

Of course, GM's subsidiary vigorously joined the anti-Jewish movement required of leading businesses serving the Reich. Jewish employees and suppliers became *verboten*. Established dealers with Jewish blood were terminated, including one of the largest serving the Frankfurt region. Even long-time executives were discharged if Jewish descent was detected. Those lower-level managers with Jewish wives or parentage who remained with the company did so stealthily, hiding and denying their background.

To conceal American ownership and reinforce the masquerade

that Opel stood as a purely Aryan enterprise, Sloan and Mooney, beginning in 1934, concocted the concept of a "Directorate," comprised of prominent German personalities, including several with Nazi Party membership. This created what GM officials themselves termed a "camouflage" or "a false facade" of local management. It seemed like GM's business in Germany was decided in Germany. But in fact the decisions were all made in America. GM, as the sole stockholder, controlled Opel's board and the corporate votes.

Among the decisions made in America beginning in about 1935 was the one transferring to Germany the technology to produce the modern gasoline additive tetraethyl lead, commonly called "ethyl," or leaded gasoline. This allowed the Reich to boost octane that provided better automotive performance by eliminating disruptive engine pings and jolts. Better performance meant a faster and more mobile fighting force—just what the Reich would ultimately need for its swift and mobile Blitzkrieg.

As early as 1934, however, America's War Department was apprehensive about the transfer of such proprietary chemical processes. In late December 1934, as GM was considering building leaded gasoline plants for Hitler, DuPont Company board director Irénée du Pont wrote to Sloan: "Of course, we in the DuPont Company have always recognized the propriety and desirability of closely cooperating with the War Department of the United States. …In any case, I know that word has gone to the War Department and have the impression that they would be adverse to disclosure of knowledge which would aid Germany in preparing that chemical." The profits, argued du Pont, were simply not worth it.

Sloan had already bluntly told du Pont, "I do not agree with your reasoning to this question." Days later, Sloan appended that GM's commercial rights were "far more fundamental... than the question of making a little money out of lead in Germany."

GM moved quickly—in conjunction with its close ally Standard Oil—to get the *Wehrmacht* the important gasoline additives. Standard and GM each took a one-quarter share of the Reich ethyl operation, while I.G. Farben, the giant German chemical conglomerate, controlled the remaining 50 percent.

The Reich's ethyl plants were built. The Americans supplied the technical know-how. Captured German records reviewed decades later by a U.S. Senate investigating committee found this wartime admission by the Nazis: "Without lead-tetraethyl, the present method of warfare would be unthinkable."

Years after the war, Nazi armaments chief Albert Speer told a congressional investigator that Germany could not have attempted its September 1939 Blitzkrieg of Poland without the performance-boosting additive.

Within a few years of partnering with the Hitler regime, Opel began to dwarf all competition. By 1937, GM's subsidiary had grown to triple the size of Daimler-Benz and quadruple that of Henry Ford's fledgling German operation, known as Ford-Werke. By the end of the 1930s, Opel was valued at $86.7 million, which in 21st-century dollars, translates into roughly $1.1 billion.

In the meantime, GM was increasingly responsible for stunning growth in Germany's economy. As most economists of the day knew, and as Sloan himself bragged, automobile manufacturing created thousands of factory jobs, hundreds of suppliers, numerous dealerships, widespread motorization and an attached oil industry.

Moreover, the growth of the highway network, from local roads to the Autobahn, necessitated by GM's vehicle manufacturing, spurred a construction boom that spawned thousands of additional jobs and required hundreds of additional suppliers. Even GM's own sponsored expert historian, who decades later examined Hitler-era documentation, concluded: "The auto industry spearheaded the remarkable recovery of the German economy that boosted the popularity of the Nazi regime by virtually eliminating within a few years the mass unemployment that had idled a quarter of the workforce and contributed so importantly to Hitler's rise."

Ironically, as thirsty as GM was for Nazi business, Reich currency restrictions obstructed the outflow of cash for profits or even the purchase of raw materials to build trucks. GM in America circumvented those regulations through the overseas sales of German pencils, sewing machines, Christmas tree ornaments and virtually any other exports that would earn foreign currency internationally.

Those sales proceeds were then exchanged for profits or raw materials through complicated bank transfers.

Ironically, while GM's Opel was a deferential corporate citizen in Nazi Germany, going the extra mile to comply with Reich requirements and making no waves, Sloan helped foment unrest at home as part of the company's efforts to undermine the Roosevelt administration.

For example, the GM president was one of the central, behind-the-scenes founders of the American Liberty League, a racist, anti-Semitic, pro-big business group bent on rallying Southern votes against Roosevelt to defeat him in the 1936 election. The American Liberty League arose out of a series of private gatherings organized in July, 1934, by Sloan, du Pont and other businessmen. Some of those meetings were even held at GM's office in New York.

The businessmen behind the hate movement sought to create a well-financed, seemingly grass-roots coalition that du Pont declared should "include all property owners... the American Legion and even the Ku Klux Klan." Sloan served on the American Liberty League's national advisory board and was one of a number of wealthy businessmen who each quietly donated $10,000 to its activities. The American Liberty League, which raised more money in 1935 than the National Democratic Party, in turn, funded an array of even more fanatical, racist and anti-Jewish groups.

One such group funded by the American Liberty League was the Southern Committee to Uphold the Constitution. With help from the du Pont family fortune, the Southern Committee circulated what it called "nigger pictures" of Eleanor Roosevelt with African-Americans. Sloan sent a $1,000 check directly to the Southern Committee after those pictures were distributed.

Racist diatribes found in Southern Committee literature included an anti-union screed that complained: "White women and white men will be forced into organizations with black African apes whom they will have to call 'brother' or lose their jobs." The Southern Committee also jointly organized protest marches with the American Nazi "Silver Shirts."

The American Liberty League also financed the Sentinels of

the Republic. The Sentinels of the Republic, in turn, orchestrated incendiary, anti-Semitic letter-writing campaigns, and otherwise provoked a backlash against Roosevelt and what was sometimes derisively labeled his "Jew Deal."

True, the Sentinels of the Republic bore all the earmarks of a rabble-rousing extremist group. But behind it were some of the nation's most affluent and well-heeled, supplying the operating cash and direction. Among them: Sun Oil President Howard Pew, investment banker Alexander Lincoln, who served as the group's president, and the president of Pittsburgh Plate Glass, John Pitcairn. Sloan himself wrote yet another $1,000 check directly to the Sentinels of the Republic.

Only after an April 1936 congressional investigation was Sloan's financial involvement in the Sentinels made public. Just days after the disclosure, Sloan issued a statement to an inquiring Jewish newspaper in Louisville, promising, "Under no circumstances will I further knowingly support the Sentinels of the Republic." He added, ambiguously: "I have no desire to enter into any questions involving religious or political questions."

Although Sloan backed away from further financing of the Sentinels, the GM chief continued to personally fund and organize fundraising for another anti-Roosevelt-agitation group, the National Association of Manufacturers. Founded in 1895 as a pro-business organization and still prominent more than 100 years later, NAM sowed anti-union and anti-New Deal discord among Americans in the 1930s through clandestinely owned and operated opinion-molding arms.

Roosevelt openly acknowledged that Sloan, GM, the du Ponts and other corporate giants hated him for his reforms and his efforts to relieve Depression-era inequities. In his final 1936 campaign speech, the president threw down the gauntlet, shouting to an overflow Madison Square Garden crowd, "They are unanimous in their hate for me—and I welcome their hatred." Roosevelt added that he wanted his first four years to be remembered as an administration where "the forces of selfishness and of lust for power met their match."

Fearing Roosevelt's possible re-election, several of Sloan's top executives at GM actually considered deliberately extending the financial woes of the Depression, presumably in retaliation against the entire nation. In the final days of the 1936 election campaign, several GM officials met with W.H. Swartz, a Lehman Brothers investment banker.

The GM officials apparently planned to stop investing in and expanding their own company in the event of Roosevelt's expected victory. Swartz's Nov. 4, 1936 confidential memo about the GM meeting asserted, "Certain General Motors people also felt further capital expenditures could not be expected now, in view of Roosevelt's possible re-election." Based on their plans, Swartz predicted "a break in general business next year ... mid-summer is the logical time to expect it," adding, "I would suggest that the rather intense political emotions of certain of these men may have colored their thinking more than they themselves may have realized."

Despite lush opposition funding by Sloan and other affluent anti-New Deal nemeses, Roosevelt was re-elected by a landslide.

While no capital slow-down was actually implemented by GM, Sloan did continue to battle the administration. The conflict was not subtle. Washington knew that Sloan and GM were powerful adversaries. For example, in 1937, when Sloan telephoned Secretary of Labor Francis Perkins to renege on a promise made to meet with labor strikers, Perkins lashed out bitterly at the GM chief.

Shocked at the reversal, Perkins shouted into the phone, "You are a scoundrel and a skunk, Mr. Sloan. You don't deserve to be counted among decent men...You'll go to hell when you die... Are you a grown man, Mr. Sloan? Or are you a neurotic adolescent? Which are you? If you're a grown man, stand up, and be a man for once." A flabbergasted Sloan protested, "You can't talk like that to me! You can't talk like that to me! I'm worth 70 million dollars and I made it all myself! You can't talk like that to me! I'm Alfred Sloan."

Even as Sloan fought the American leadership during the late 1930s, General Motors' German automotive subsidiary, Opel, remained a loyal corporate citizen of the Third Reich—content to obediently do the Nazi regime's bidding, and unstintingly supporting Hitler's program on many fronts. These included economic and employment recovery, anti-Jewish persecution, war preparedness and domestic propaganda. In return, Opel prospered.

Hitler was pleased with GM—very pleased. In 1938, just months after the Nazis' annexation of Austria, James D. Mooney, head of GM's overseas operations, received the German Eagle with Cross, the highest medal Hitler awarded to foreign commercial collaborators and supporters.

During November 9-10, 1938, shortly after Mooney's decoration, nationwide pogroms broke out in Germany against the Jews —Kristallnacht. The American public was finally shocked onto its heels by the night of officially orchestrated burning, looting and mob action again Jews. President Roosevelt recalled America's ambassador, plunging German-American relations to their lowest point since Hitler assumed power. Now all things American came under special scrutiny in Germany.

By now, especially after *der Führer's* medal to Mooney, the truth about GM's ownership of the Opel car and truck operation was out in the open among Germans. Reich armament officials increasingly directed Opel's output, including mandating that nearly all vehicles be devoted to military use. That was exactly what Sloan wanted—a pivotal and profitable place in the war everyone was expecting.

In the tense months leading up to the feared 1939 invasion of Poland, Sloan defended his close collaboration with Hitler. Brushing off attacks for his partnership with a Nazi regime already notorious for filling concentration camps, taking over Austria and now threatening to install the Master Race across Europe, Sloan was stony and proud. He stated, in a long April 1939 letter to an objecting stockholder, that GM shouldn't risk alienating its German hosts and Reich profits by intruding in Nazi affairs. "In other words, to put the proposition rather bluntly," Sloan said in the letter, "such matters should not be considered the business of the management of General Motors."

Indeed, in August of 1939, the world wondered exactly when Hitler might invade Poland. GM knew. During those days, Opel, under the direct day-to-day supervision of GM's senior executive, Cyrus Osborn, played a key role in Germany's fast-paced military plans. The company was already manufacturing thousands of Blitz trucks that would become a mainstay of the Reich's upcoming *Blitzkrieg.*

The German military in early August urgently ordered Blitz truck spare parts to be delivered to Reich bases near the Polish border. Days later in August, nearly 3,000 Opel employees, from factory workers to senior managers, were drafted into the *Wehrmacht.* Moreover, at about that time, GM's Osborn began evacuating most of the American employees and their families to the Netherlands. Soon, virtually all Opel civilian passenger car sales were eliminated in favor of military orders.

At 6 a.m. on Sept. 1, 1939, Germany launched its *Blitzkrieg* against Poland, with troops arriving in Blitz trucks manufactured by GM's Opel. The night before, Sloan told stockholders that GM was "too big" to be impeded by "petty international squabbles."

Shortly after war broke out in Europe, however, GM executives in Germany tried to distance the American company from its involvement in the brutal German war machine. The Opel board was restructured to ensure that GM executives maintained a controlling presence on the board of directors but continued invisibility in daily management. This was accomplished in part by bringing in GM's reliable Danish chief, Albin Madsen, and maintaining two Americans on that board.

The company's 1939 annual report, released in April 1940, stated: "With full recognition of the responsibility that the manufacturing facilities of Adam Opel A.G. must now assume under a war regime, the Corporation has withdrawn the American personnel formerly in executive charge... and has turned the administrative responsibilities over to German nationals."

However, GM was still masquerading. By the summer of 1940, a senior GM executive wrote a more honest assessment for internal circulation only. He explained that while "the management of Adam Opel A.G. is in the hands of German nationals," in point of fact, GM is still "actively represented by two American executives on the Board of Directors."

The German-American balance of the many management entities constructed to create a facade of control constantly shifted
during the Hitler years. But regardless of the number of members
—German or American—on the various directing, managing or
executive boards and committees, GM in the United States controlled all voting stock and could veto—or permit—all operations.

Once war began, for all intents and purposes, *Wehrmacht*
requirements and orders determined the specifics of military manufacturing at Opel. Like any nation at war, including the United
States itself, the Reich alone determined what weapons would be
made by its militarized factories. That said, it was GM's decision to
remain operating in Germany, to continue to subject itself to Reich
military orders, and answer the Reich's call for ever more lethal
weapons.

As anticipated, Opel's Brandenburg facilities were conscripted
and converted to an airplane engine plant supplying the Luftwaffe's
JU-88 bombers. Later, Opel's plants also built land mines and torpedo detonators. The factories and infrastructure that GM built
during the 1930s was in fact finally used for their intended purpose
—war. Opel-built trucks on the ground, Opel-powered bombers in
the sky, and Opel-detonated torpedoes in the seas brought terror to
Europe from every direction.

Back in the United States, Sloan tried to obstruct FDR's war
preparedness planning. The GM chief tried to dissuade GM executives with needed manufacturing and production experience from
helping Washington's early mobilization plans. In one typical 1940
case, Sloan asked Danish-born William Knudson, who had ascended
to become president of GM, not to leave the company and help
Washington's war efforts. Sloan, who had become chairman of the
company in 1937, warned his friend that the Roosevelt administration would make a "monkey out of you."

Knudson replied, "That isn't important, Mr. Sloan. I came to
this country [from Denmark] with nothing. It has been good to
me. Rightly or wrongly, I feel I must go." Sloan retorted, "That's a
quixotic way of looking at it."

By mid-1940, with or without Sloan's acquiescence, GM had

been drafted by Washington to become a major war supplier for the Allies. Sloan had no choice but to comply, and GM and its employees would ultimately make enormously valuable contributions to the Allied war effort.

In June 1940, Sloan brought Mooney back to America to head up GM's key participation in America's crash program to prepare for war. He was installed as an assistant to the new GM president to take "full charge of all negotiations [with Washington] involving defense equipment."

Mooney's mere appointment sent shivers through the anti-Nazi boycott and protest committee, which well remembered his 1938 medal for what the Nazis had termed "service to the Reich." The Non-Sectarian Anti-Nazi League railed in a letter to Roosevelt: "How should we interpret the placing of a Hitler sympathizer and a Hitler servant (one must render service to the Reich to deserve such a medal) at the throttle of our defense program? Doesn't that appear suspiciously similar to the planting of Nazi sympathizers in key positions?"

In June 1940, about the same time Mooney returned to America, Sloan wrote to a colleague, expressing disdain for FDR's democracy while grudgingly acknowledging his admiration for Hitler's fascist drive, even if that drive had become criminal.

"It seems clear that the Allies are outclassed on mechanical equipment," Sloan wrote, "and it is foolish to talk about modernizing their Armies in times like these, they ought to have thought of that five years ago. There is no excuse for them not thinking of that except for the unintelligent, in fact, stupid, narrow-minded and selfish leadership which the democracies of the world are cursed with."

Sloan added a poignant contrast, "But when some other system develops stronger leadership, works hard and long, and intelligently and aggressively—which are good traits—and, superimposed upon that, develops the instinct of a racketeer, there is nothing for the democracies to do but fold up. And that is about what it looks as if they are going to do."

When at the end of 1940 the White House began to insist that

GM break off relations with Latin American car dealers suspected of being pro-Nazi, Sloan defiantly refused. He lashed out at Washington, accusing it of protecting Communists at home while focusing on GM dealers in South America. "I have flatly declined to cancel dealers," Sloan wrote in April 1941 to Walter Carpenter, a GM board member and vice president of du Pont.

Days later, on April 18, 1941, Carpenter retorted, "I think that General Motors has to consider this problem from three standpoints; first, from the commercial, second, the patriotic and, third, the public relations standpoint....We are definitely a part of the nation here and our future is very definitely mingled with the future of this country. The country today seems to be pretty well committed to a policy opposite to Germany and Italy."

Carpenter continued with a blunt warning. "If we don't listen to the urgings of the State Department in this connection," he said, "it seems to me just a question of time... The effect of this will be to associate the General Motors with Nazi or Fascist propaganda against the interests of the United States...The effect on the General Motors Corporation might be a very serious matter and the feeling might last for years."

A few weeks later, in May 1941, by now 18 months after World War II broke out, Sloan, then in his mid-60s, began to speak in bewildering terms about the GM-Hitler axis. With newspapers and newsreels constantly transmitting the grim news that millions had been displaced, murdered or enslaved by Nazi aggression and that London was decimated by the Blitz bombing campaign, Sloan told his closest executives during a Detroit briefing: "I am sure we all realize that this struggle that is going on though the world is really nothing more or less than a conflict between two opposing technocracies manifesting itself to the capitalization of economic resources and products and all that sort of thing."

He then continued in a rambling, incoherent fashion, trying to further justify the company's Nazi business dealings.

By now, Assistant Secretary of State Adolf Berle, whose portfolio included the investigation of Nazi fronts and sympathizers in Latin America, had enough of Sloan and GM executives. Berle circulated a memo asserting "that certain officials of General Motors were sympathetic to or aligned with some pro-Axis groups....this is [a] 'real Fifth Column' and is much more sinister than many other things which are going on at the present time." Berle called for an FBI investigation.

The FBI's probe of GM senior executives with links to Hitler found collusion with Germany by Mooney, but no evidence of any disloyalty to America. The August 2, 1941 summary of the investigation clearly listed Sloan in the title of the report, but Mooney's was the only name mentioned in the investigative results. However, in a separate report to FBI director J. Edgar Hoover, the agent stated, "No derogatory information of any kind was developed with respect to Alfred Pritchard Sloan Jr."

On December 7, 1941, Pearl Harbor was bombed. The United States declared war on Japan. On December 11, German diplomats in Washington called at the State Department to deliver Germany's declaration of war against America. All direct communications between GM and its Opel subsidiary in Germany were necessarily severed, although indirect links remained through Denmark where GM operated a longtime subsidiary. Ranking GM men from Denmark were also in key positions both in Opel in Germany and GM in America.

After Germany declared war on America, all American corporate interests in Germany or under German control were systematically placed under the jurisdiction of a Reich-appointed "custodian" for enemy-owned property. In practice, the "custodian" was akin to a court-appointed receiver. Generally, the Reich custodian's duty was not to dismember the firm or Aryanize it, but to continue to run the enterprise as efficiently and profitably as possible, holding all assets and profits in escrow until matters would be resolved after the war. This generally meant re-appointing members of the pre-existing management team, although these managers no longer reported directly to their American masters in the United States.

In the case of Opel, Carl Luer, the longtime member of the Opel Supervisory Board, company President and Nazi Party stalwart, was appointed by the Reich to run Opel as "custodian." Luer was only so designated, but some 11 months after America entered the war. Indeed, in anticipation of the outbreak of hostilities, GM had appointed Luer to be president of Opel in late 1941, just before war broke out. He merely remained in place.

In other words, the existing GM-approved president of Opel continued to run Opel during America's war years.

The company continued as a major German war profiteer, and GM knew its subsidiary was at the forefront of the Nazi war machine. An August 27, 1944 *New York Times* article detailed that Opel was the principal target of a 1,400-plane RAF bombing mission because its 35,000-worker plant was turning out crucial military transport and was known to be developing rocket technology.

In the wartime months and years that ensued, 1941-1945, GM also built and operated some $900 million worth (about $120 billion in today's dollars) of defense manufacturing facilities for the Allies. Almost all of the company's undertakings were propped up by federal programs that guaranteed profit and "cost-plus" contracts, various subsidies, tax benefits and other incentives then available to defense contractors to produce goods for the war effort. Secretary of War Henry Stimson later explained that when a capitalist country wages war, "you have got to let business make money out of the process, or business won't work." General Lucius Clay, who oversaw war materiel contracts, confessed, "I had to put into production schedule the largest procurement program the world had ever seen. Where would I find somebody to do that? I went to General Motors."

To be sure, GM cleverly reaped the financial benefits of its relationship with the Third Reich as well. During the pre-war Hitler years, GM entered its Opel proceeds under "reserves" instead of listing the profits as ordinary income. Then during America's war years, GM declared it had "abandoned" its Nazi subsidiary; the company took a complete tax write-off under special legislation signed by Roosevelt in October 1942. The write-off of nearly $35 million created a tax reduction of "approximately $22.7 million" or about $285 billion in 21st-century money, according to an internal Opel document.

But Opel's friendly Nazi custodian, Luer, kept on making profits for the company during those war years. Opel produced trucks, bomber engines, land mines, torpedo detonators and other war materiel, a significant amount of it produced by the sweat of thousands of prisoner laborers or other coerced workers. Some of those workers were tortured if they did not meet expectations. Those profits and GM's 100 percent stock ownership were preserved by the Reich custodian, even though GM and Opel ostensibly "severed ties" with each other after America entered the war.

During the Hitler years, many of those excess profits were used to acquire other companies and properties, only increasing Opel's assets in Germany. After the war, starting in 1948, GM began regaining control over Opel operations and eventually its monumental assets as well as blocked dividends. GM also collected some $33 million in "war reparations" because the Allies had bombed its German facilities.

After the defeat of Berlin, GM and its executives, including those who joined the government in Washington, then steered America toward its gargantuan postwar boom. That boom was in large measure powered by the constellation of direct and indirect economic benefits delivered by the U.S. automobile industry.

Ironically, while GM was mobilizing the Third Reich, the company was also leading a criminal conspiracy to monopolistically undermine mass transit in dozens of American cities that would help addict the United States to oil.

The war in Europe had only been over for 16 months when on October. 2, 1946, a memo from the Department of Justice landed on the desk of J. Edgar Hoover, outlining the elements of the GM conspiracy.

At the center of the conspiracy was National City Lines, a shadowy company that suddenly arose in 1937, ostensibly run by five barely-educated Minnesota bus drivers, the Fitzgerald brothers. Yet the Fitzgeralds miraculously marshaled millions of dollars to buy up one failing trolley system after another. Soon, through a patchwork of subsidiaries, the brothers owned or controlled transit systems in more than 40 cities. Generally, when National City Lines acquired the system, the tracks were pulled from the street, the beloved electric trolleys were trashed or burned, and the whole system was replaced with more expensive, unpopular and environmentally hazardous motor buses that helped addict America to oil.

The Justice Department discovered that National City Lines was just a front company for General Motors, in league with Mack Truck, Phillips Petroleum, Standard Oil of California and Firestone Tires—all petroleum interests. The companies became the major preferred stockholders of National City Lines but operated behind the scenes.

The scheme worked this way: The manufacturers purchased NCL preferred stock to acquire transit lines on condition that when the systems were acquired, the trolleys would be dismantled and replaced with motor buses. That is exactly what happened. All the conspirators gained immensely when non-polluting electric systems were replaced by oil-burners. Phillips and Standard sold the petroleum products. Firestone sold the tires. GM and Mack divvied up the bus manufacturing and sales market according to an agreed-upon formula.

Transit systems in 16 states were converted, adversely affecting millions of Americans, who had to pay higher fares for lesser, more unpopular service. Dozens more cities were targeted in the $9.5 million scheme.

In April 1947, indictments alleging two counts of criminal conspiracy were handed down against General Motors, Mack Truck, Phillips Petroleum, Standard Oil of California and Firestone Tires, as well as against numerous key executives of the companies.

The defendants were found guilty on one of the two counts: conspiring to monopolize the bus business by creating a network of petroleum-based transit companies that were forbidden to use transportation or technology products other than those supplied by the defendants themselves. This criminal conspiracy effectively banned electric transit. The jury found the defendants not guilty on the second count alleging a conspiracy to actually control those transit systems.

On April 1, 1949, the judge handed down his sentence: a

$5,000 fine to each corporate defendant except Standard, which was fined $1,000. As for National City Lines, President E. Roy Fitzgerald and his co-conspirators at GM and the other companies, they too were fined. Each was ordered to "forfeit and pay to the United States of America a fine in the amount of one dollar."

The cases were appealed—even the one-dollar penalties—all the way to the United States Supreme Court, which allowed the convictions to stand. The government filed a civil action against the same circle of companies trying to stop their continued conduct. But the government was unsuccessful. Undaunted, National City Lines and its many subsidiaries continued into the 1950s to acquire, convert, and operate urban transit systems using evolved methods.

*****

In an unusual epilogue to the tumultuous saga of General Motors during the New Deal and Nazi era, the company continued making history by attempting to suppress its history.

A generation after World War II, in 1974, the company's controversial conduct was resurrected by the U.S. Senate Judiciary Committee's subcommittee on Antitrust and Monopoly. GM and Opel's collusion with the Nazis dominated the opening portion of the subcommittee's exhaustively documented study, which mainly focused on the company's conspiracy to monopolize scores of local mass transit systems in the United States.

The report's author, Judiciary Committee staff attorney Bradford Snell, used GM's collaboration with the Third Reich as a moral backdrop to help explain the automakers' plan in more than 40 cities, to subvert popular, clean-running electric public transit and convert it to petroleum-burning motor buses.

The Senate report, titled "American Ground Transport," was released shortly after the Arab-imposed 1973 oil shock — and it accused GM of significantly contributing to the nation's petroleum woes through its mass-transit machinations. After Snell's report was presented, GM immediately went on the counterattack, denying Snell's charges about both its domestic conduct and its collusion with the Nazis, and demanding that the Senate Judiciary Committee cease circulating its own report. That, of course, did not happen.

But following the release of the Snell report, the automaker then created its own 88-page rebuttal report titled, "The Truth About American Ground Transport," whose entire first section, as it turns out, had nothing to do with American ground transport. It was headlined: "General Motors Did Not Assist the Nazis in World War II."

Thus, GM's involvement with Nazi transportation in Germany juxtaposed with its conspiracy to convert electric mass transit at home became inextricably linked by virtue of the Senate's investigation, the company's own rebuttal and the compelling historical parallel between the company's conduct in the United States and its conduct in Germany.

Going further, GM demanded that the Senate never permit American Ground Transport, its own report, to be distributed without GM's rebuttal attached. In a rare move, the Senate agreed. Snell, however, labeled the GM rebuttal a document calculated to mislead historians and the public.

Yet another generation later, in the late 1990s, GM's collaboration with the Nazis was again resurrected when Nazi-era slave laborers threatened to sue GM and Ford for reparations. At the time, a GM spokesman told a reporter at *The Washington Post* that the company "did not assist the Nazis in any way during WWII." The effort to sue GM and Ford was unsuccessful, but both Ford and GM, concerned about the facts that might come to light, commissioned histories of their Nazi-related past.

In the case of Ford, the company issued its 2001 report, compiled by historian Simon Reich, plus the original underlying documentation, all of which was made available to the public without restriction. Ford immediately circulated CDs with the data to the media. Researchers and other interested parties may today view the actual documents and photocopy them. The Reich report concluded, among other things, that Ford-Werke, the company's German subsidiary, used slave labor from the Buchenwald concentration camp in 1944 and 1945 and functioned as an integral part of the German war machine. Ford officials in Detroit have publicly commented on their Nazi past, remained available for comment, apologized, and have generally helped all those seeking answers about its involvement with the Hitler regime.

As for GM, in 1999 it commissioned controversial business historian Henry Ashby Turner Jr. to conduct an internal investigation and report his findings. Turner, author of several books, including *German Big Business and the Rise of Hitler*, was well known, among other things, for his insistence that big business did not make a pivotal contribution to the rise of Hitlerism. He had also garnered a reputation for using his position and a vicious letter-writing campaign to hound another junior historian out of the profession because he had written about the pivotal role of big business in the Third Reich.

Turner produced his internal report, but GM declined to release it. GM has maintained a special combative niche in the annals of American corporate history, achieving a reputation for suppressing books, obstructing access to archival records and frustrating critics from Ralph Nader to Bradford Snell. GM attorneys even fought efforts by Alfred P. Sloan himself to publish his memoirs, although the autobiography was finally published in 1964 after a long court fight.

In July 2005, Turner published his own book *General Motors and the Nazis: The Struggle for Control of Opel, Europe's Biggest Carmaker*. The book features 158 text pages of carefully detailed and footnoted information, plus notes, an index, and a short appendix. More than a year later, BookScan, which tracks about 70 percent of retail book sales for the publishing industry, reported that only 139 copies of the Turner book had been sold to the key outlets monitored by the service since the publication's release.

In his book, Turner, relying on his work as GM's historian, disputed many earlier findings about GM's complicity with the Nazis, concluding that charges that GM had collaborated with the Nazis even after the United States and Germany were at war "have proved groundless." Turner rejects "the assumption that the

American corporation did business in the Third Reich by choice," asserting, "Such was not the case." Turner also stated that GM had no option but to return wartime profits to its stockholders, since "the German firm prospered handsomely from Hitler's promotion of the automobile and from the remarkable recovery of the German economy."

However, Turner does state explicitly that "by the end of 1940 more than ten thousand employees at Opel's Russelsheim plant were engaged in producing parts for the Junkers bombers heavily used in raining death and destruction on London and other British cities during the air attacks of the Battle of Britain." In addition, Turner condemns GM for taking Opel's wartime dividends, which included profits made from slave labor. He writes, "...regardless of who [in the GM corporate structure] decided to claim that tainted money, its receipt rendered GM guilty, after the fact, of deriving profit from war production for the Third Reich made possible in part from the toil of unfree workers."

* * * * *

Unquestionably, GM's impact during the Hitler era, both in the United States and the Third Reich, was monumental. Without GM, Hitler would have never had the motorized ability to conquer Europe and mechanize the dispossession and destruction of numberless Jewish communities.

On January 15, 1953, company president Charlie Wilson was nominated to be Secretary of Defense, a job that would ultimately see him usher in the era of the interstate highway system. At Wilson's confirmation hearings, Sen. Robert Hendrickson (R-N.J.) pointedly challenged the GM chief, asking whether he had a conflict of interest, considering his 40,000 shares of company stock and years of loyalty to the controversial Detroit firm. Bluntly asked if he could make a decision in the country's interest that was contrary to GM's interest, Wilson shot back with his famous comment, "I cannot conceive of one because for years I thought what was good for our country was good for General Motors, and vice versa. The difference did not exist. Our company is too big."

Indeed, what GM accomplished in both America and Nazi Germany could not have been bigger.

Sources: Primary documentation for this chapter are mainly drawn from *Internal Combustion: How Corporations and Governments Addicted the World to Oil and Derailed the Alternatives* by Edwin Black and a special 4-part syndicated JTA investigation titled *Hitler's Carmaker*, as well as a review of documents at Georgetown University; Georgia State University; Henry Ford Museum; Kettering University; National Archives repositories in Chicago and Washington, D.C.; New York Public Library Special Manuscript Collections; Yale University Sterling Memorial Library and other repositories in the United States and Germany. Additional documentation arose from confidential FBI files obtained under the Freedom of Information Act and period media reports from both Germany and America. Secondary literature consulted included the books, *General Motors and the Nazis* by Henry A. Turner; *Sloan Rules* by David Farber and *Working for the Enemy* by Reinhold Billstein, Karola Fings, Anita Kugler and Nicholas Levis.

CHAPTER FIVE

IBM Organizes the Holocaust

Everything within was dark, illuminated this moonlit night only by the desperate eyes and drawn faces of dozens of petrified Jews who had been loaded into the boxcar. Most stood, some squatted if they could. A few could not help but lie on the floor, some in their own defecation. The train sounded like a piston cycling. It swayed rhythmically as it sped toward Treblinka.

Edjya, a thin, twelve-year-old girl sat quietly on the boxcar floor, listening to the thudding rail ties, trying to understand the stream of terrible events befalling her family. Her mother nudged and whispered, "You're a skinny one, Edjya, always a skinny one," as she anxiously eyed the tiny vent at the top of the cattle car.

"Quickly, up there," she said suddenly. "Edjya, go through." Her mother repeated urgently, "Quickly, I said."

Two men nearby pulled and pulled until the first wooden slats broke. Piece by piece, they yanked it until the entire grille was off, allowing a slender portal of escape.

"Up now. Up!" they commanded, as they hoisted Edjya upon their shoulders. As the train rocked, the men lifted Edjya's legs through first, then forced her protruding hips, and pushed some more until she rested on her stomach, half in, half out of the speeding boxcar.

"We'll let you down slowly. Hold onto the towel," her mother said.

Edjya inched out of the vent and down the horizontal wooden slats of the boxcar's exterior until her elbows and then finally her wrists, cleared. Now with one foot resting on an exterior bolt, and hanging onto the towel against the wind, Edjya cried out in terror, "Take me back up. I can't do it."

"Get ready," her mother instructed. "When you hit the ground, run, Edjya, run. And tell someone. Tell someone what is happening."

* * * * *

But someone—or rather one company—did know what was happening to Edjya, her family, and indeed all the Jews of Europe during the Holocaust.

When the Nazis identified exactly where Jews lived, even those living Christian lives but with Jewish ancestors in their bloodlines, one company knew what was happening. When the Reich persecution machine pinpointed exactly which professors, doctors, art dealers and members of any of a thousand other niches in society were Jews, and then ousted them, one company knew. When the banks seized Jewish savings, corporate stock and property, one company knew. When the Jews were rounded up in Frankfurt, Warsaw, and hundreds of other cities and meticulously squeezed into ghettos or concentration camps, one company knew. When the Nazis burst into a Polish or Hungarian town with all the Jews listed, numbered, and alphabetized, demanding that the named ones present themselves, one company knew. When Jews with skills were suddenly plucked from their enslavement in one part of occupied Europe and transferred to another camp where those skills were needed—and then worked to death, one company knew. When the Jews, catalogued by numbers and scheduled by precise calculations, were herded into trains and metered into death camps, one company knew.

Who knew? Answer: International Business Machines and its

president, Thomas J. Watson. IBM organized and essentially co-planned the Holocaust with the Nazis.

How did it work? Long before the information age, going back to the nineteenth century, IBM controlled information technology by virtue of punch card technology. Punch card systems, the fore-runners of computers, could capture any type of information in the holes punched into the rows and columns of a specially prepared paper card. When a machine "read" the card, names, addresses, and other personal data were revealed according to the punched holes. Originally designed for censuses as a "people identifier," punch cards were quickly adapted for any number of statistical and informational purposes. By correctly setting up the informational input, punch cards could also reveal any data about trains, ware-house goods, sales, financial transactions, and indeed anything or any process that lent itself to statistics, tabulation, or tracking.

A government census employee named Herman Hollerith invented the punch card system during the 1880s for the U.S. Census Bureau. This system allowed the Bureau to gather vastly more census information then ever before, and assemble the results in weeks and months, not years as previously required. Hollerith then stole the government's technology to found his own company. That company evolved into the international conglomerate known as IBM.

Throughout the first half of the twentieth century, the names IBM and "Hollerith" were synonymous and generic for each other and punch card technology. Hence, IBM tabulators were called "Hollerith machines," IBM punch cards were called "Hollerith cards," and IBM bureaus were commonly referred to as "Hollerith Bureaus." Prior to the advent of Hollerith, the world had never seen such an ability to track and organize its citizens and activities.

In the hands of Adolf Hitler, a new era was born. For the first time in history, people were not just numerically counted. A whole constellation of data about the counted individuals, how they inter-faced into society, and how society interfaced with them, could be swiftly tabulated, assembled, and analyzed. The Third Reich reacted to its information with lightning speed, and constantly asked for more. Hence, 1933 Berlin saw the dawn of the Information Age, that is, the individualization of statistics.

With IBM as a partner, the Hitler regime was able to substantially automate and accelerate all six phases of the twelve-year Holocaust: identification, exclusion, confiscation, ghettoization, deportation, and even extermination. For IBM, Hitler's Reich represented an immense source of profit. Indeed, from the first moments of its strategic relationship with Germany, beginning in 1933, the Reich became IBM's largest overseas customer.

As it did with any other customer, IBM simply asked the Hitler regime what result was wanted. Then company engineers devised custom-tailored punch card systems to deliver the results. IBM billed itself as "The Solutions Company." It was an identity the firm never lost. There was no solution IBM was unwilling to provide.

The first solution the Reich wanted was to quickly identify exactly who was Jewish, exactly where the Jews lived, and exactly which professions they worked in. What's more, among the approximate 600,000 Jews in Germany, the Reich wanted to identify first the so-called "Eastern Jews," that is, the Jews from Eastern Europe. Hitler reviled these Jews the most.

Under the continuous micromanagement of IBM's obsessive president Thomas J. Watson, himself a corporate criminal previously convicted in a massive extortion conspiracy, the company constructed a solution.

IBM in New York instructed its German subsidiary to design a massive German census, one which the firm would actually execute with its own employees and equipment. Special punch cards were designed by IBM engineers to identify the Jews, their origin, current location, and profession. Working hand-in-hand with the Nazis, a massive, door-to-door national census was undertaken throughout Germany in 1933. The key was not only gathering the information on paper forms with answers to the key questions organized into "fields," but then punching the precise information into the correct location on punch cards especially created for the purpose. This required IBM engineers to design and print millions of compatible punch cards and paper forms, assemble and train an army of secretaries to punch in the data, and deliver large numbers of machines—sorters and tabulators—and ensure that the settings could read the data properly. Finally, IBM had to produce the clear, printed results that the Nazis desired.

Each census answer was assigned a number and a position on the punch card. New York rented a giant building in Berlin for the prodigious tabulating project. By punching religion in one column, nationality in another column, native language in a third column, city in a fourth column and then profession in its own column, at the rate of 24,000 cards per hour, IBM could identify exactly—for example—how many Jews of Polish extraction were engaged in the fur trade in Berlin.

Beyond the census, numberless police registrations, marriage bureaus, labor certificates and other statistical points also recorded information about religion and nationality. Like census data, the information often began with paper and pencil, but then wended its way into Hollerith systems housed at various statistical offices throughout the Reich.

Despite the data dragnet, many simply did not know they had Jewish blood in their ancestry. In many cases, parents or grandparents had converted to Christianity decades before, as was common in extremely assimilated German Jewish society. But eventually, these people were also identified as Jews by old church baptismal books, conversion certificates, genealogical records, birth and death notices, and eugenic agency findings that were increasingly used to update or check against IBM data records. In many instances, the records of these other agencies were punched into their own databases which were then cross-tabulated.

The Nazis were amazed.

But identification was just the first step. IBM explained to Nazi officials that their subsequent requests and the new anti-Jewish programs being quantified were limited to the column and row technology of the existing punch card and its machine readers. There was no use gathering information or recording processes that could not be tabulated. In other words, the state of the technology was both an enabling and a limiting factor. As such, each informational, statistical, analytical or tracking step the Nazis took was planned in partnership with IBM to achieve maximum efficiency. In turn, IBM regularly improved its machines to work faster, father, yield more information, and eventually alphabetize. The Reich was an insatiable customer. Nazi Germany had insatiable demands.

Once Germany's Jews were indentified, the second solution the Nazis sought was to effectively oust them from every segment of society. Lawyers, judges, doctors, teachers, merchants, traders, government officials, journalists, musicians, employees of all types, even members of organizations such as auto clubs and gardening groups were all caught up in the cross-comparison of directories, membership books, rosters and other lists. Lists, lists, lists. If you were a Jew on a list, you were expelled from your profession or terminated from your employment. Increasingly, these lists were IBM tabulated or cross-checked against other IBM tabulations.

So many bewildered Jews asked: where did Hitler get the names? Answer: IBM.

IBM's custom-built tabulating machines were never sold to the Nazis, just leased. The company was paid monthly—right through the war years. IBM in New York maintained strict control over the location and use of their machines. Each was insured in Hartford Connecticut, whether the machine was housed on IBM property in Germany or a Nazi office. Hence information about location, application and risk environment, including war risk, was always needed.

Millions of custom-designed punch cards were printed under almost clinical conditions to guarantee the not-too-flexible not-too-rigid quality needed for the clackety-clack of IBM tabulators. IBM produced them using its own specialty presses according to a patented process. To ensure its primacy, the New York office sued any firm in any country that tried to print its own cards or even print a competitive brand. A card could only be used one time as it passed through the machinery and yielded its punched information. Once used, a punched card was fully expended, like a fired bullet. Therefore millions upon millions of additional cards were continuously printed for the Reich. The need for custom-printed

Hollerith cards was a seemingly inexhaustible profit center for the company.

Moreover, IBM engineers and designers were in constant demand. No "standard" card existed. Some featured 10 columns and rows, some had 20, and others offered a "double 40" configuration. Each application needed a special Hollerith card freshly-designed by IBM for its client, whether that client was Hitler's government, the Nazi Party, the German military, or the many agencies and companies embedded within the Third Reich. Each such card project was designed by IBM as a hand-notated mock-up and after being approved by Nazis, was it placed into mass production. The IBM subsidiary in question always proudly imprinted its name along the edge.

What's more, the precision tabulators, sorters, and printers needed careful cleaning and servicing every two to four weeks. That was done with unstoppable regularity, regardless of where the machines were deployed. To perform the required maintenance, IBM repairmen visited their machines on site, whether in a bustling suburb of Berlin or a grisly concentration camp such as Auschwitz.

The third solution the Nazis needed was to pauperize the Jewish community. In Hitler's view, Jews had stolen all their money and owed the German state for their biologically inferior presence. Jewish-owned bank accounts, insurance policies, stock holdings, real estate and other assets could be systematically identified because IBM bureaus serviced nearly all the banks, savings institutions, brokerages and taxing authorities. Once Jews were identified, it became a mere cross-tabulation and data mining operation to locate Jewish assets. IBM customer service men helped expedite the process. Step-by-step, Jewish assets were liquidated by Nazis as they exacted special fines, flight taxes, penalties, deposits, Aryanization, and outright confiscation. Many Jews rushed to hide their assets. But all too often, IBM systems eventually found them.

Ghettoization was the fourth solution the Nazis sought. Here IBM engineers devised data programs to match addresses of Jews in ordinary residential neighborhoods against ghetto relocation addresses where five, six, and seven families were cruelly packed into a single, dilapidated flat. Herding Jews into ghettos was not a free-for-all. It was all organized. On moving day, every evicted Jewish family was assigned a ghetto building and apartment number. IBM machines, using programs specifically created for the purpose, calculated the population transfers in advance. Once the people were moved in, the Nazis walled them in. Now the Jews were trapped.

When it came time for the fifth solution, systematically deporting the Jews into concentration camps, again IBM was there. Hollerith systems ran all the trains. Before punch cards were applied to the railroad industry, it could take weeks to locate a boxcar and transport it from place to place. With IBM punch cards, the process was orderly and highly efficient. The exact number of trains running the exact number of needed boxcars was calculated for the exact number of ghetto Jews to be deported to the concentration camps with capacity. Special IBM programs were devised to meter the Jews from ghetto to camp. It worked like clockwork because IBM worked hard to automate the process.

Throughout the Reich years, millions of people from all nationalities, religions and ways of life were transported in and out of numerous Nazi concentration camps and scores of subcamps. Yet the one-day capacity of all concentration camps combined on most days was approximately 500,000. That daily level of traffic management was only made possible with IBM efficiency.

*****

Who at IBM knew? How was the New York headquarters involved in the Reich's minute-to-minute dependence upon IBM, and who approved it all? Was the Reich-IBM axis implemented by low-level employees or subsidiaries acting without New York's knowledge? It was the opposite. The entire business relationship with the Third Reich was approved by company president Thomas J. Watson, who ruled the company's many overseas subsidiaries with an iron-fist and micromanaged their daily activities. Watson maintained a 5 percent bonus on every dollar of after-tax, after-dividend IBM business with the Reich. So he had a personal stake in every transaction.

Who was Watson? He was a salesman—a born salesman. All born salesmen know that the addicting excitement of a sales victory is short-lived. No matter how great the sale, it is never enough. Selling, for such people, becomes not an occupation, but a lifestyle. Any salesman can sell anything. Every salesman alive knows these words are true. But they also know that not all salesmen can go further. Few of them can *conquer*. Watson was a conqueror. He conquered a sales territory the way a general would invade and occupy a nation.

Quickly, Watson learned that some sales positions offered something called a *commission*, that is, a cut. At age 21, he joined the National Cash Register Company, where he helped head a secretive conspiracy of extortion and deception to drive innocent cash register competitors out of business. His work involved establishing front companies, creating phony transactions and hiding the details from all but the top echelons of the company. Watson and others were prosecuted and in 1913 convicted by a federal jury in Ohio, although on appeal Watson was able to get his conviction overturned on an evidence technicality.

He went on to join the company that would later change its name to International Business Machines. He promised to run IBM with the same vigor he showed at National Cash Register. Watson insisted on his "cut" of all business. At IBM, Watson imbued his blue-suited shock troops of sales, many of whom were involved with overseas subsidiaries, to ignore all issues of politics and persecution, overlook any disagreements with the conduct of foreign governments, and focus on the almighty sale. In defense of Fascism, Watson made clear, "Different countries require different forms of government and we should be careful not to let people in other countries feel that we are trying to standardize principles of government throughout the world."

Indeed, IBM conducted business with governments in scores of countries, including virtually every nation in Europe. For this, IBM maintained wholly-owned subsidiaries or licensees across the Continent. In Germany, the wholly-owned IBM subsidiary was Deutsche Hollerith Maschinen Gesellschaft—the German Hollerith Machine Corporation, or *Dehomag* for short. IBM acquired Dehomag, originally a licensee, after Germany's post-World War I hyperinflation and economic collapse. Watson kept on Dehomag company founder Willy Heidinger with a vague promise of a 20 percent profit-sharing agreement. Tension between Heidinger, a rabid Nazi, and Watson was continuous as Heidinger tried to collect on Watson's promises of compensation. But the money was somehow always blocked by a clever Watson, who understood that every dollar spent reduced his own bonus.

Watson was consulted before any business decision or major expenditure was taken. It was not uncommon to check with him before painting a corridor in a German office, soliciting a government agency in Austria, or delivering a promised tabulator to a client. Watson insisted on approving the smallest details.

At the same time, Watson had learned painfully from his earlier fraud conviction, which in large measure rested upon highly incriminating writings and documents. With a world condemning Germany for its vicious anti-Semitic campaigns, brutality, and threats of war against its neighbors, Watson insisted that, as much as possible, the company deal with the Reich via untraceable oral agreements. During the pre-war Reich years, Watson personally visited Germany several times annually to oversee operations and convey instructions in person. Late in the 1930s, in anticipation of war breaking out, Watson found it easier to pass instructions through the company's office in Geneva, Switzerland, thus maintaining a degree of deniability amid horrific war news, and circumventing U.S. law severely restricting commerce with the Reich.

War did break out on September 1, 1939 when Germany invaded Poland. News of barbarous massacres, rapes, inflicted starvation, systematic deportations, and the resulting unchecked epidemics made headlines around the world. Jews in particular were mercilessly brutalized. Shortly after the war began, a *New York Times* article headlined "250,000 Jews Listed as Dead in Poland."

Polish Jewry numbered more than 3 million persons—10 percent of the Polish population. Atrocities, rapes, and massacres could not wipe them all away. Deportation to labor camps was underway.

But something more drastic was needed. Extermination was being discussed, privately and publicly.

A German military review of specific actions in Poland declared, "It is a mistake to massacre some 10,000 Jews and Poles, as is being done at present... this will not eradicate the idea of a Polish state, nor will the Jews be exterminated." On September 13, the *New York Times* reported the Reich's dilemma with a headline declaring, "Nazis Hint Purge of Jews in Poland," with a subhead, "3,000,000 Population Involved." The article quoted the German government as declaring it wanted "removal of the Polish Jewish population from the European domain." The *New York Times* then added, "How... the 'removal' of Jews from Poland [can be achieved] without their extermination... is not explained."

The Nazis needed the newest IBM alphabetizers to more efficiently organize the elimination of Polish Jewry. With the tumultuous outbreak of World War II in the background, Dehomag manager Herman Rottke in Berlin carefully wrote to Watson, asking him to accelerate delivery of the new machines for both Germany and those still in recently annexed Austria.

September 9, 1939
Mr. Thomas J. Watson, President
International Business Machines Corporation
590 Madison Ave.
New York, NY USA

Dear Mr. Watson:

During your last visit in Berlin at the beginning of July, you made the kind offer to me that you might be willing to furnish the German company machines from Endicott in order to shorten our long delivery terms. I... asked you to leave with us for study purposes one alphabetic tabulating machine and a collator out of the American machines at present in Germany. You have complied with this request, for which I thank you very much, and have added that in cases of urgent need, I may make use of other American machines...

You will understand that under today's conditions, a certain need has arisen for such machines, which we do not build as yet in Germany. Therefore, I should like to make use of your kind offer and ask you to leave with the German company for the time being the alphabetic tabulating machines which are at present still in the former Austria... Regarding the payment, I cannot make any concrete proposals at the moment, however, I should ask you to be convinced that I shall see to it that a fair reimbursement for the machines left with us will be made when there will be a possibility....

[A]t the time that the German production of these machines renders it possible, we shall place at your disposal... a German machine for each American machine left with us. This offer, made orally by you, dear Mr. Watson... will undoubtedly be greatly appreciated in many and especially responsible circles... We should thank you if you would ask your Geneva organization, at the same time, to furnish us the necessary repair parts for the maintenance of the machines...

Yours very truly,
H. Rottke
cc: Mr. F. W. Nichol, New York and IBM Geneva

IBM's alphabetizer, principally its model 405, was introduced in 1934, but it did not become widely used until it was perfected in conjunction with the Social Security Administration. The elaborate alphabetizer was the pride of the company. Sleek and more encased than earlier Holleriths, the complex 405 integrated several punch card mechanisms into a single, high-speed device. A summary punch cable connector at its bottom facilitated the summarizing of voluminous tabulated results onto a single summary card. A short card feed and adjacent stacker at the top of the machine was attached to a typewriter-style printing unit equipped with an automatic carriage to print out the alphabetized results. Numerous switches, dials, reset keys, a control panel, and even an attached reading table, made the 405 a very expensive and versatile device. By 1939, the squat 405 was IBM's dominant machine in the United States. However, the complex statistical instrument was simply too expensive for the European market. Indeed, in 1935, the company was still exhibiting it at business shows. Because the 405 required so many raw materials, including rationed metals that Dehomag could not obtain, IBM's alphabetizer was simply out of reach for the Nazi Reich.

But the 405 was of prime importance to Germany for its critical ability to create alphabetized lists and its speed for general tabulation. The 405 could calculate 1.2 million implicit multiplications in just 42 hours. By comparison, the slightly older model 601 would need 800 hours for the same task—fundamentally an impossible assignment.

More than one thousand 405s were operating in American government bureaus and corporate offices, constituting one of the company's most profitable inventions. But few of the expensive devices were anywhere in Europe. Previously, Dehomag was only able to provide such machines to key governmental agencies directly from America or through its other European subsidiaries—a costly financial foreign exchange transaction, which also required the specific permission of Watson.

Now that Germany had taken over Poland and war had been declared in Europe, such imports from America were no longer possible. But Dehomag wanted the precious alphabetizing equipment still in Austria by the pre-war IBM subsidiary. The Austrian set included five variously configured alphabetical punches, two alphabetical interpreters, and six alphabetical printing tabulators, as well as one collator. However, these valuable assets were still owned and controlled by the prior IBM subsidiary in Austria. Moving these to Dehomag's control required Watson's permission.

A tendentious written exchange ensued, in part using undated letters—even if their filing date stamps used by clerical staff remained clear. Some of the letters were passed through Geneva via secretaries and go-betweens. J. W. Schotte, IBM's newly promoted European general manager in Geneva, acted as Watson's intermediary on the alphabetizer question. On September 27, 1939, the day a vanquished Warsaw formally capitulated, Schotte telephoned Rottke and the Dehomag management team in Berlin to regretfully explain that Watson refused to transfer the alphabetizers without further negotiation on sales territory, including asking the German unit to service Russia. Dehomag bristled at taking on more territory than was profitable too soon.

Both sides negotiated the economics and Reich necessity. Schotte called Rottke the next morning, September 28, "in friendly spirits." Watson had seen the business wisdom of consolidating the efforts of the Austrian and German efforts under Dehomag.

Dehomag's paperwork, approved personally by Watson, was quickly finalized:

> **Alphabetical Summary Punch...serial #517-10674-D9**
> *Transferred to Dehomag*
> **Alphabetical Summary Punch...serial #517-10072**
> *Transferred to Dehomag*
> **Alphabetical Duplicating Printing Punch...serial #034-11722-M8**
> *Transferred to Dehomag*
> **Alphabetical Duplicating Punch...serial #034-11252**
> *Transferred to Dehomag*
> **Alphabetical Duplicating Punch...serial #034-11253**
> *Transferred to Dehomag*
> **Alphabet-Interpreter...serial #552-10494-C9**
> *Transferred to Dehomag*
> **Alphabet-Interpreter...serial #552-10495-C9**
> *Transferred to Dehomag*
> **Alphabetical Printing Tabulating Machine...serial #405-13126-D9**
> *Transferred to Dehomag*
> **Alphabetical Printing Tabulating Machine...serial #405-13127-D9**
> *Transferred to Dehomag*
> **Alphabetical Printing Tabulating Machine...serial #405-13128-D9**
> *Transferred to Dehomag*
> **Alphabetical Printing Tabulating Machine...serial #405-11332**
> *Transferred to Dehomag*

Alphabetical Printing Tabulating Machine...serial #405-11000
  Transferred to Dehomag
Alphabetical Printing Tabulating Machine...serial #405-10206
  Transferred to Dehomag
Collator...serial #077-10577-D9
  Transferred to Dehomag

* * * * *

Clearly, once war had broken out, the Nazis wanted one more solution, a final solution. IBM gave it.

Nearly every Nazi concentration camp operated an IBM customer site, the Hollerith Department known in German as the *Hollerith Abteilung*. The three-part Hollerith system of paper forms, punch cards, and tabulators, varied from camp to camp and from year to year, depending upon conditions. In some camps, such as Dachau and Storkow, as many as two dozen IBM sorters, tabulators, and printers were installed. Other facilities operated punches only and submitted their cards to central locations such as Mauthausen or Berlin. In some camps, the plain paper forms were coded and processed elsewhere.

Hollerith activity—whether paper, punching, or processing, was frequently located within the camp itself, consigned to a special bureau called the Labor Assignment Office, known in German as the *Arbeitseinsatz*. The *Arbeitseinsatz* issued the all-important daily work assignments and processed all inmate cards and labor transfer rosters. This necessitated a constant barrage of lists, punch cards, and encodeable documents as every step of the prisoner's existence was regimented and tracked.

Hitler's Reich established camps all over Europe, but they were not all alike. Some, such as Flossenbürg in Germany, were labor camps where inmates were worked to death. Several, such as Westerbork in Holland, were transit camps, that is, staging sites *en route* to other destinations. A number of camps, such as Treblinka in Poland, were operated for the sole purpose of immediate extermination by gas chamber. Some camps, such as Auschwitz, combined elements of all three.

Without IBM's machinery, continuing upkeep and service, as well as the supply of punch cards, whether located on-site or off-site, Hitler's camps could have never managed the numbers they did.

IBM engineers assigned Hollerith code numbers for each of the major camps:

Auschwitz ... 001
Buchenwald ... 002
Dachau ... 003
Flossenbürg ... 004
Gross-Rosen ... 005
Herzogenbusch ... 006
Mauthausen ... 007
Natzweiler ... 008
Neuengamme ... 009
Ravensbrück ... 010
Sachsenhausen ... 011
Stutthof ... 012

Auschwitz, coded 001, was not a single camp, but a sprawling complex, comprised of transit facilities, slave factories and farms, gas chambers, and crematoria. In most camps, the *Arbeitseinsatz* tabulated not only work assignments, but also the camp hospital index, and the general death and inmate statistics for the Political Section. For example, in August 1943, a timber merchant from Bendzin, Poland, arrived at Auschwitz among a group of 400 inmates, mostly Jews. He was registered by Hollerith method in the labor index for the *Arbeitseinsatz* and assigned a characteristic five-digit Hollerith number: 44673. This five-digit IBM number would follow the Polish merchant from labor assignment to assignment as Hollerith systems tracked him and his availability for work, and reported it to the central inmate file, which was eventually kept at Department DII. Department DII of the SS Economics Administration in Oranienburg oversaw all camp slave labor assignments.

Later in the summer of 1943, the timber merchant's same five-digit Hollerith number, 44673, was tattooed on his forearm. Eventually, during the summer of 1943, all non-Germans at Auschwitz were similarly tattooed. The infamous Auschwitz tattoo began as an IBM number.

Tattoos, however, quickly evolved at Auschwitz. Soon, they bore no further relation to Hollerith compatibility for one reason: the Hollerith number was designed to track a working inmate—not a dead one. Once the daily death rate at Auschwitz climbed, Hollerith-based numbering simply became outmoded. Clothes would be quickly removed from any cadaver, making identification for the Hollerith-maintained death lists difficult. So camp numbers were inked onto a prisoner's chest. But as the chest became obscured amidst growing mounds of dead bodies, the forearm was preferred as a more visible appendage. Soon, *ad hoc* numbering systems were inaugurated at Auschwitz. Various number ranges, often with letters attached, were assigned to prisoners in ascending sequence. Dr. Josef Mengele tattooed his own distinct number series on patients. Tattoo numbering ultimately took on a chaotic incongruity all its own as an internal Auschwitz-specific identification system.

But Hollerith numbers remained the chief method Berlin employed to centrally identify and track prisoners at Auschwitz. For example, in late 1943, some 6,500 healthy, working Jews were ordered to the gas chamber by the SS. But their murder was delayed for two days as the Political Section meticulously checked each of their numbers against the Section's own card index. The Section was under orders to temporarily reprieve any Jews with traces of Aryan parentage as part of Germany's eugenic protocol.

Sigismund Gajda was processed by the three-step Hollerith system. Born in Kielce, Poland, Gajda was about 40 years of age when on May 18, 1943, he arrived at Auschwitz. A paper form, labeled "Personal Inmate Card," recorded all of Gajda's personal information. He professed Roman Catholicism, had two children, and his work skill was marked "mechanic." The reverse side of his Personal Inmate Card listed nine previous work assignments. At the bottom of the Card's front panel was a column to list any physical punishments meted out, such as flogging, tree-binding, or beating. Once Gajda's card was processed, a large indicia in typical Nazi Gothic script letters was rubber-stamped at the bottom: "*Hollerith erfasst,*" or "Hollerith registered." That IBM designation was stamped in large letters on hundreds of thousands of processed Personal Inmate Cards at camps all across Europe.

Auschwitz' print shops produced the empty plain paper Personal Inmate Cards for Hollerith operations utilized at most other concentration camps. Sometimes the Auschwitz presses simply could not keep up with demand. In one instance, on October 14, 1944, the leader of Ravensbrück's Hollerith Department sent a letter to his counterpart at Flossenbürg's Hollerith Department confirming that a work gang of 200 females had been dispatched for slave labor at the Witt Company in Helmbrechts. "The inmates' personal cards as well as the Hollerith transfer lists are being submitted," the Ravensbrück officer leader wrote. But, he added, "Since at the moment, no [Inmate] Cards can be obtained from the Auschwitz printers, temporary cards had to be made for that part of the transport."

All Auschwitz inmate information, including workers still alive, deaths and transferees, was continuously punched into the Hollerith system servicing the camp. Tabulated totals were wired each day to the SS Economics Administration and other offices in Berlin by the various camp Hollerith Departments. Hollerith tracking was the only system for monitoring the constantly shifting total population of all camps.

The "Central Inmate File" at the SS Economics Administration was a mere paper file, but all its information was punched into the central Hollerith banks in Berlin and Oranienburg. Each prisoner was tracked with a single paper card boldly labeled at the top *Häftlingskarte*, that is, "Inmate Card." That paper card was filled with personal information handwritten in fields next to the corresponding Hollerith code numbers to be punched into IBM equipment. No names were used to identify prisoners in this file—only their assigned Hollerith numbers. Each five- or six-digit number was coupled with a concentration camp number. Hence, each camp could potentially register 999,999 inmates.

For instance, one nameless inmate was assigned the six-digit number, 057949, which was to be punched into columns 22 and

27 of a Hollerith card. He was born on October 7, 1907, which was punched into section 5. The Criminal Police, which was coded 1 in column 2, took the man into custody in the town of Metz, which was punched into a different row. November 11, 1943 was his arrest date, which was punched into section 3. Prisoner 057949 was marked as a Communist Spaniard, coded 6 for column 4. As a male, box 1 for column 6 was checked; but since he was unmarried, box 1 for column 7 was also checked; his one child necessitated an additional mark for column 8. Prisoner 057949 was transferred to Dachau, coded "03" for columns 21 and 26.

Along the bottom of Prisoner 057949's card was a series of lines for each concentration camp to which he was assigned. At the right of each camp entry line was a grid marked *Holl. Verm.* for "Hollerith Notation" above two separates boxes: one marked "In," and the next marked "Out."

At the bottom right of every Inmate Card was a special processing section labeled *Kontrollvermerk*. Under *Kontrollvermerk* were three boxes:

> *ausgestellt* for "issued"
> *verschlüsselt* for "encoded"
> *Lochk. geprüft* for "punch card verified."

The punch card operator's number was hand-stamped in the "punch card verified" box to maintain quality control. Millions of identical Inmate Cards were run through the system, all featuring column-numbered data fields, the distinctive "Hollerith Notation" grid, and control boxes to certify the punch card processing details. When a number holder deceased, his number was simply re-issued. Of the millions produced, more than a hundred thousand such Inmate Cards survived the war.

Hollerith tracking worked so well that the SS Economics Administration was able to authoritatively challenge the slave labor reports they were receiving on any given day. For instance, at one point in the latter part of 1943, the central office asked for the number of Auschwitz Jews fit for reassignment to an armaments plant. On August 29, Auschwitz replied that only 3,581 were available. Senior SS Economics Administration Officer Gerhard Maurer knew from DII's Hollerith sorts that fully 25,000 Jews were available for work transfers. Four days later, Maurer dispatched a brash rejoinder to Auschwitz Camp Commandant Rudolf Höss himself. "What are the remaining 21,500 Jews doing?" Maurer demanded. "Something's amiss here! Please again scrutinize this process and give a report."

Hollerith Departments at camps could not be operated by miscellaneous labor whether they used mere coded paper forms, cards, or actual machines. They required so-called Hollerith experts trained by IBM in Germany, or any of the other countries depending upon location. At Auschwitz, the Hollerith managers were located in the "Hollerith Buro" in the Auschwitz III camp complex, also known as Monowitz. The building was near the I. G. Farben factory. The Hollerith Buro's telephone number, 4496, was published in the Auschwitz phone book on page 50.

Buchenwald, coded 002, was established in July 1937, long before the war started. From its inception, Buchenwald was a cruel destiny for Germany's social undesirables, including politicals, hardened criminals, so-called work-shy misfits, Jehovah's Witnesses, homosexuals, and Jews. The Hollerith system was needed from the outset to code and segregate each type of inmate, and then ensure the prisoner was subjected to a regimen of maltreatment and deprivation prescribed for his category.

Ironically, when many Jews, homosexuals, and Jehovah's Witnesses registered at Buchenwald, they were required to write "career criminal" on the front of their "Personal Inmate Card" as a welcoming humiliation ritual. Their real occupation was noted on the back. Those who balked at listing themselves as criminals were severely beaten.

So many hundreds of thousands of IBM cards, all with the characteristic red IBM subsidiary logo printed along the edge, clicked through the Hollerith machines of Buchenwald, and its many sub-camps, that spent cards were typically cut in half so the backs could be used for note pads. For example, the flip side of a punch card recording production details at the Zwieberge sub-camp was re-used to request shift assignments. The commander scribbled on the back: "please deploy Alfred and Schneider to *Kommando 1*. They are to be transferred to a shift… in Block 12."

Deaths were so numerous at Buchenwald that the hospital staff jotted individual details on the back of used IBM cards. Typically, the deceased inmate's five-digit or six-digit number, sometimes with barracks number appended, was scrawled next to the name and nationality, next to two dates: entry into the hospital and death. German Prisoner 52234 entered April 11 and died April 12. French prisoner 71985 entered on April 14 and exited on April 15. French Jewish prisoner 93190 entered April 14 and departed two days later. A telltale array of punched holes was always clearly visible on these square scraps.

Dachau, coded 003, was the Reich's first organized concentration camp, established in March 1933, in the first weeks of the Hitler regime. Several detention camps had been erected early on. But Dachau, set up just 10 kilometers from Munich, was the first Nazi camp created to inflict hellish cruelty on the Reich's undesirables, especially Communists and Jews. Offices of the merciless *Waffen*-SS and its predecessor organizations were located at Dachau. *Waffen*-SS units were militarized SS troops that actively participated in some of the bloodiest murders of the war. They utilized at least four multi-machine sets of IBM machines, including IBM's most advanced.

While Dachau was originally established for Germans, once the Reich conquered Europe, inmates from many countries were processed through its Hollerith machines. Middle class Parisian prisoners were in abundance. Prisoner 072851, a French salesman, was taken by the Security Police in Paris; Hollerith operator number 8 processed his card. Prisoner 072850, a chef, was also taken by the Security Police in Paris; Hollerith operator number 8 also processed his card. Prisoner 072833 was a gardener, taken by Security Police in Paris; Hollerith operator 8 punched his information as well. The very next card in the sequence belonged to Prisoner 072834, a baker taken by Security Police in Paris; that card was punched by Hollerith operator 9.

The IBM machines at Dachau were housed in a bomb-proof

blockhouse called the "Hollerith Bunker," located directly across from the main gate. The company's equipment was managed by several Hollerith experts and non-technical supervisors. Albert Bartels, head of the SS punch card agency, with no particular expertise, functioned as the senior official. Herbert Blaettel possessed the technical knowledge since he was a former IBM subsidiary dealer in Germany and later worked in the subsidiary's training department. Blaettel was aided by Heiber, considered a virulent SS man. Busch, another technical expert, had been a Dehomag dealer since 1932 and finally joined the SS in 1943 to help the SS operate its machines. Dachau received IBM's very first advanced alphabetizer, the DII-A.

Flossenbürg, coded 004, was another camp built in Germany before the war. The giant facility, built near the town of Floss, continuously worked inmates to death at a nearby granite quarry and Messerschmitt aircraft factory. When enfeebled prisoners by the thousands dropped dead from malnutrition and exhaustion, their bodies were quickly cremated.

Because Flossenbürg was primarily a slave labor camp, it relied heavily on Hollerith machines to coordinate the work battalions transferring in and out from other major camps or its own sub-camps. The camp's well-developed Hollerith Department tracked its slaves by name and number. During September 1944, thousands of prisoners were transferred to Flossenbürg proper from its smaller sub-camps.

On September 1, 1944, for example, Flossenbürg's Hollerith Department received secret notice #1049/44, specifying that six of those sub-camps were transferring a total of 2,324 cards corresponding to the attached "Hollerith Transfer Lists." From Camp Neurohlau: 561; from Camp Zwodau: 887; from Camp Graslitz: 150; from Holleischen: 603; and from Camp Helmbrechts: 100. Seventeen women were also transferred to a special Flossenbürg detachment. The secret notice to Flossenbürg's Hollerith Department explained: "The inmates' files have been kept in the records of the local camps up until and including August 31, as was already reported by telegram. The transfer lists for the Hollerith card file are attached as well."

Notice #1049/44 to Flossenbürg also stressed that although 2,324 cards were accompanying the Hollerith transfer printouts, six women had escaped during the past few months. "The inmates' files have been removed from the records of local camps, after their escape," the notice instructed, "and their records have to be reinserted into the files upon their capture." The six women were listed by name and Hollerith number:

#22941 Basargina, Elena

#30279 Baranecka, Lena

#29306 Saganjatsch, Nadia

#23021 Edwokimenko, Diana

#28803 Krlanisch, Valentina

#34434 Hildinberg, Gertrud

Printouts from Flossenbürg's Hollerith Department were used to organize and accompany the transfer not only of large slave groups numbering more than 1,000, but small work gangs as well. On January 24, 1945, Flossenbürg's *Arbeitseinsatz* received notice from another camp's Hollerith Department: "We are submitting inmate personal cards for 200 inmates transferred to work camp Helmbrechts and 200 inmates transferred to work camp Dresden... Hollerith lists are included." Several months before, on September 1, 1944, Flossenbürg's *Arbeitseinsatz* received a similar order but for half as many inmates. "In the attachment," the September 4, 1944 notice informed, "find enclosed the inmate personal cards for 100 inmates transferred to work camp Witt in Helmbrechts on August 31, 1944. The Hollerith transfer list is included."

Hollerith lists could be produced for as few persons as needed. On November 13, 1944, Flossenbürg's *Arbeitseinsatz* received orders involving just four women: "The inmate personal cards for 4 female inmates transferred to work camp Helmbrechts on November 9, 1944, as well as Hollerith transfer list Number 123 are submitted in the attachment. We are requesting the speediest delivery of personal file cards for the 4 transferred inmates."

Among the many punch card operations in concentration camps, perhaps the most active was the massive Hollerith Department at Mauthausen. The giant Austrian camp was an extensive complex of slave labor quarries and factories, operated with a brutal furor, calculated to quickly work inmates to death. Sadistic labor conditions amid unspeakable daily atrocities killed thousands. Numerous Mauthausen sub-camps functioned as satellites in a similar vein. Moreover, as camps consolidated late in the war, captives were continuously shipped into the camp so Mauthausen received many transfers from other facilities. Hollerith operators located in the *Arbeitseinsatz*, across from the Political Section, could see the entire parade grounds, including the arrival of every prisoner transport.

A low-level SS officer supervised Mauthausen's Hollerith Department. But day-to-day sorts and tabulations were undertaken by a Russian-born French army lieutenant POW named Jean-Frederic Veith. Veith arrived at Mauthausen on April 22, 1943, just days before his fortieth birthday. He was quickly assigned to the tabulators. Among Veith's duties was processing the many Hollerith lists from other camps, not only transferred prisoners for new assignment, but those the sorts had determined were misrouted.

Veith compiled both the voluminous death lists and new arrival rosters, and then dispatched the daily "strength numbers" to Berlin. His section stamped each document *Hollerith erfasst*—Hollerith registered, and then incorporated the figures into the camp's burgeoning database. Hence, the enormity of Mauthausen's carnage was ever-present in his mind as he ran the machines.

Mauthausen "Departure Lists" were fundamentally roll calls of the dead. A typical handwritten "Departure List" ran on for many pages, 30 lines per page. No names were used, just the inmate's five-digit or six-digit Hollerith identity, listed on the left in numerical order for efficient punching into column 22 of the IBM cards printed for camp death tallying. The victim's birth date was penned into the next table for punching into section 5. Death dates were scrawled in the right field set aside for section 25.

Cause of death was recorded for column 24. Generally, the murdered inmate itemized on the top line was coded C-3, the Hollerith designation for "natural causes." For convenience, ditto marks signifying "natural causes" would then be dashed next to every inmate number. But these death citations were faked. For amusement, Mauthausen guards often forced an inmate to jump off the quarry cliff at a spot called "the Parachute Jump." Exhausted laborers might also be crowded into the tiled gas chamber below the sick bay where carbon monoxide billows would suffocate their lives. Undesirables might be terminated in "Operation K" actions—a bullet administered at close range. Or special cases might be hoisted by their arms tied behind their backs until they died from the socket-wrenching excruciation. All these murders were almost always dittoed C-3, "natural causes."

The Hollerith installations at Auschwitz, Buchenwald, Dachau, and Mauthausen were only part of an extensive network of camp sorting, punching and tabulating services that stretched across Europe. At Stutthof camp in Poland, coded 012, the Hollerith Department used six-digit registrations beginning with zero. At the nightmarish Gusen camps, the Hollerith cards were not only set up to record personal biographical and work assignments, they also recorded the gruesome details of painful punishments administered to prisoners, such as floggings and hanging from a tree with arms bound in back. For Westerbork transfer camp in Holland, Hitler's Holleriths were used to schedule efficient trainfuls of prisoners destined for Auschwitz gas chambers, and then report the numbers back to the registration office.

At Bergen-Belsen, where surviving prisoners were described by liberators as "emaciated apathetic scarecrows huddled together in wooden huts," the Hollerith cards were maintained in a barracks dubbed "the lion's den," located in the *Arbeitseinsatz*. To obliterate all evidence of the mass murders documented by the Hollerith records, Himmler ordered all camp card indices to be destroyed before the Allies arrived.

At Ravensbrück woman's camp, IBM coded 010, the busy Hollerith Department used its own "Ravensbrück" rubber stamp to save time writing. Punch card operators at Ravensbrück often identified their work by letter, rather than number. A stream of Hollerith transfer lists always accompanied Ravensbrück slave women transported to various factory sites and camps. One could live as long as one could work. Ravensbrück women always knew fellow prisoners were about to be exterminated when a trusty abruptly retrieved their cards. One British inmate recalled in a secret letter written at the time, "The selected ones have to wait in front of the Block... while the [trusty]... who has noted their numbers goes to the *Arbeitseinsatz* and gets their cards (which are only removed if the prisoner is dead). An hour later she returns with the cards and a lorry and they go—never to return."

The SS Economics Administration, under the leadership of *Gruppenführer* Oswald Pohl, utilized Hollerith systems for more than specific prisoner tracking. IBM machinery helped the SS manage the massive logistics of the entire camp system. Jews from across Europe were being continuously transported into the camps. At the same time, slaves within camp confines died or reached the limits of their utility to the Reich. The prodigious task of efficiently scheduling deportation from cities and ghettos in many countries, the daily work assignments, and outright extermination timetables would have been impossible without the daily strength reports. When the camps reached the maximum of even their inhumane overcrowded capacity, orders went out from Berlin to reduce the density. Those periodic orders issued by the SS Economics Administration were based on the well-honed statistics provided by the Holleriths both in the camps and at camp administration headquarters.

In fact, a special statistical bureau was eventually established in January 1944 to coordinate and tabulate all new registrations, death lists, daily strength reports, and transfers from site to site. This virtually unknown secret punch card facility was simply called *Zentral Institut*, that is, the Central Institute. Each day, camps would forward copies of their strength reports to *Zentral Institut*, located on a quiet, residential street in Block F at 129 Friedrichstrasse in Berlin.

Although the location was tranquil, the traffic in and out was constant. Couriers delivered weekly "Departure Lists" from the various camps. For example, Mauthausen's list for week 37 of 1944 was six pages long—virtually all deceased. For week 40, the list was seven pages long. For week 41, it was six pages, recording 325 deaths. For week 44, seven pages listed 369 prisoners. An October 17, 1944 delivery of prisoner cards from Mauthausen's Hollerith Department included data on 6,969 males and 399 females.

Zentral Institut was able to render the big picture only because it processed the most individualized details. For instance, on January 2, 1944, the SS officer in charge of Mauthausen's Hollerith Department informed his counterparts at Flossenbürg's Hollerith Department about three named and numbered prisoners who had recently transferred in. One died in transport and two others were utilized in an unspecified secret project. Since they were never actually registered at Mauthausen, the Hollerith Department suggested their names just be sent to *Zentral Institut* as "departures."

Zentral Institut's elaborate Hollerith banks at Block F, 129 Friedrichstrasse were expensive systems. But the SS could more than justify the cost because slave labor was sold by the SS Economics Administration and managed as a profit center. Enterprises as large as the heavy industries of I.G. Farben, as delicate as Hotel Glasstuben, and as small as a local business, routinely contracted for slave labor with Department DII, which governed all slave labor assignments. For instance, in late July 1942, farmer Adam Bär of Würzelbrunn, short on farmhands for his beet fields, applied to DII for two farm slaves from Flossenbürg.

The SS Economics Administration, which had total operational control of all camps, could supply exactly the skilled workers required and transfer people from camp to camp, and factory to factory, by setting the dials of their Hollerith systems that had stored the details of all inmate cards. Two important inmate cards were utilized. The Personal Inmate Card was used for on-site camp registration and stayed with the individual in the field. DII's centralized version was simply called "Inmate Card." Every Inmate Card held in DII's Central Inmate File listed the prisoner's profession in a field to be punched into column 10 of the IBM card. For example, Spanish inmate 30543 was listed as a lumberman. That qualified 30543 to be assigned by the Neuengamme concentration camp as a "helper" in any slave enterprise. Occupational details for column 10 were provided by the top line of the reverse side of the Personal Inmate Card.

Maschinelles Berichtwesen, the Reich's central punch card agency, had helped develop the slave labor punch card in conjunction with Dehomag engineers. These cards listed inmates by nationality and trade. After matching any of the millions of slaves and conscripted workers, both in camps and incoming foreign labor battalions, to the numerous requests by both private companies and public works, DII could promptly deploy workers where they were needed, when they were needed. In this sense, DII acted like any worker placement agency.

Charges for DII's workers could be easily tabulated on Dehomag's well-established hourly wage cards, thereby generating instant slave billings. A typical monthly charge to Messerschmitt airplane works for Flossenbürg slaves was the one itemized on DII's invoice #FLO 680, which was issued December 1, 1944:

50,778 fulltime skilled slaves at RM 5 per day
5,157 part-time skilled slaves at RM 2.50 per day
53,071 fulltime helpers at RM 3 daily
5,600 part-time helpers at just RM 1.50 daily

Messerschmitt's total invoice for the month of November 1944 was RM 434,395.50. Although Messerschmitt employed 114,606 Flossenbürg slaves in November 1942, once the month closed on November 30, DII was able to generate an itemized invoice within 24 hours. Prompt payment was requested.

Slave revenues for all camps totaled RM 13.2 million for 1942. This program of working inmates to death had a name. The Reich called it "Extermination by Labor." Atop the ironwork entrances of many slave camps was an incomprehensible motto: *Arbeit Macht Frei*—"Work will set you free."

Without IBM's custom designed programs, flawlessly maintained machines, and continuous supply of millions of new punch cards, Extermination by Labor could never have been organized. It was in fact, an IBM designed and coordinated extermination program.

In addition, to coding the camps, IBM devised codes for the prisoners. Political detainees were coded 1. Homosexuals were coded 3. Gypsies were coded 12. Jews were coded 8. IBM also created punch card codes for the four most common forms of death at the camps. Death by natural causes was coded 3. Execution was coded 4. Suicide was coded 5. *Sonderbehandlung*, that is, "Special Treatment" was coded 6. "Special treatment" meant either the gas chamber or a bullet in the neck.

Hence, IBM engineers had to design an interactive system to capture information on which Jews were gassed. The company had to design the cards, have the cards printed, ensure that the Hollerith machines could read the information, train staff to punch and process the data, and service the machines to ensure they yielded the proper results. It was yet another solution for the Solutions Company. Indeed, it was IBM's final solution.

* * * * *

As the Third Reich conquered Europe, IBM moved in cadence with it, opening new subsidiaries either just before the Nazis invaded, or just after. For example, after Germany invaded Poland, the Reich annexed northwestern Poland. The remaining Polish territory in Nazi hands was treated as "occupied" and called the "General Government." That northwestern quadrant was serviced by IBM's German subsidiary, Dehomag. In annexed Poland, Dehomag mainly serviced the payroll of Silesian coal mines and heavy industry.

At about that time, IBM NY established a special new subsidiary, totally separate and apart from its German subsidiary. IBM's new Polish company was named for the president in New York. It was called Watson Business Machines. The new subsidiary's sole purpose was to service the Nazis during the rape of Poland. The enterprise would require dozens of custom-wired punch-card machines, and millions of proprietary punch cards that were specially designed and printed for each application. It remained completely legal for IBM to service the Third Reich until just before the United States entered the war in December 1941.

The Polish subsidiary, like all IBM's overseas units, was micro-managed personally by IBM president Thomas J. Watson from his office at 590 Madison Avenue in New York.

IBM began by establishing its new headquarters at 23 Kreuz Street in Warsaw. Its former Polish manager Janusz Zaporski was replaced by a Nazi, Alexander von Dehn, according to IBM's files.

Accountants and managers created a murky and confusing network across Europe. Special accounting provisions allowed the German and Polish units to overlap. When the Polish company ran out of punch cards, Dehomag could supply them by paying a commission to the Polish company. When the Polish company ran out of machines, Dehomag could supply them, but the Polish subsidiary charged a 25 percent maintenance commission. IBM's French machines brought to Poland by the German army could be rented out by the Polish branch but required a 25 percent rental commission to the German unit. When a Polish supplier wanted to return some equipment, IBM NY asked that it be shipped to the Swedish subsidiary, from where it could be credited to the Geneva office, and then to New York. To further deniability for IBM in New York, the Polish manager was given written authorization to receive money, but only an untraceable verbal authorization to actually deposit it into IBM's Account #4b at the Handlowy Bank. When the smoke cleared, it would be impossible to track which machine and which dollar belonged to which subsidiary.

A print shop for punch cards was maintained at 6 Rymarska Street, directly across the street from the Warsaw Ghetto. Indeed, the ghetto walls actually indent around IBM's print shop location. Two people were needed to run the three printing machines and one card cutter, using paper brought in from Germany. Ultimately, the shop at Rymarska produced as many as 10 million cards per year. Most of those cards were used by Polish railroads.

In 1940, to make sure the staff of Watson Business Machines was well-cared for, IBM president Thomas J. Watson told his Geneva representative P. Taylor to arrange cash grants—disguised as loans to avoid taxes—and special food packets. Bonuses were given for meeting sales quotas to Nazi clients in Poland.

The most important IBM customer site was 22 Murner Street in Krakow, the Reich's Statistical Office, where a 500-man *Hollerith Gruppe*, served by dozens of IBM Hollerith punch-card machines, calculated endless projections, such as the rate of deaths per square kilometer due to progressive starvation, and the number of Jews to be transported to the death camps. It also conducted and tabulated continuous censuses and registrations, according to the Statistics Office of the General Government.

The Statistics Office was divided into six distinct groups—Group I: Administration; Group II: Population and Culture; Group III: Food and Agriculture; Group IV: Economic Trade and Transportation; Group V: Social Statistics, and Group VI: Finance and Tax. A November 30, 1941, Statistics Office report explained, "The *Hollerith Gruppe* area of operation stretches across all subject areas," adding, "Our work is just beginning to bear fruit."

In early October 1941, IBM's general manager Werner Lier visited Berlin to oversee the movement of IBM machines across Nazi Europe. He wrote two detailed reports to Watson and senior staff indicating that he shipped a small number of Polish machines to Romania in time for the Jewish census there, according to IBM correspondence. But the Polish machines would soon be replaced by others.

The 24 Murner Street facility had already punched in 60,000 volumes of the Polish Statistical Service's census data, where it was compared with the "ethnic" data from the ghettos. Nazi Holleriths calculated exactly how many Jews could be metered out of the ghettos, either for work assignments or transport to the death camps. The exact number of boxcars and locomotives was tracked by Group IV—Transportation. The Nazis then required the ghetto councils to pick and choose names to meet quotas—or the elders would be shot. Deported Jews were subtracted from the rolls at 24 Murner Street in the on-going process.

Machine shortages were often solved by subterfuge. In 1942, after the United States entered the war, IBM president Watson dispatched his chief attorney, Harrison Chauncey, to a Berlin meeting with IBM Czech subsidiary manager Georg Schneider to secretly authorize him to place Czech machine tags on Nazi tabulators and lease them as Czech machines, according to a letter from Schneider to Watson recounting the meeting. Schneider was instructed to transmit rent disguised as royalties from Czechoslovakia to Switzerland—and then on to New York. Some of these "Czech" machines then ended up in Poland.

An important Watson Business Machines customer site was the Hollerith Department of Polish Railways, located at 22 Pawia Street in Krakow. This office kept tabs on all trains in the General Government, including those that sent Jews to their death in Treblinka and Auschwitz.

Leon Krzemieniecki is probably the only man still living who worked in that Hollerith Department. Krzemieniecki was not aware of the details of routes that would end in genocide. Indeed, his duties required tabulating information on all trains, from ordinary passenger to freight trains, but only after their arrival. The high-security five-room office, guarded by armed railway police, was equipped with 15 punchers, two sorters and a tabulator "bigger than a sofa," Krzemieniecki remembered more than a half-century later.

Fifteen Polish women punched the cards and loaded the sorters. Three German nationals supervised the office, overseeing the final tabulations and summary statistics in great secrecy. Handfuls of printouts were reduced to a small envelope of summary data, which was then delivered to a secret destination. Truckloads of the preliminary printouts were then regularly burned, along with the spent cards, Krzemieniecki recalled.

"I knew they were not German machines," recalled Krzemieniecki. "The labels were in English... The person maintaining and repairing the machines spread the diagrams out sometimes. The language of the diagrams of those machines was only in English."

Asked if the machine logo plates were in German, Polish or English, he answered "English. It said 'Business Machines.'" Asked, "Do you mean, 'International Business Machines?'" Krzemieniecki replied, "No, 'Watson Business Machines.'"

On July 4, 1945, just weeks after the war ended, the manager of IBM's Czech subsidiary, Dr. Georg Schneider, wrote a letter to

Thomas J. Watson in New York, summarizing his loyal efforts on behalf of the New York office. "I beg to give you my report about the IBM office in Prague, Czechoslovakia," wrote Schneider. "All the interests of the IBM were in good hands. The $-rentals were transferred to the account of IBM in Geneva, after begin [sic] of war with U.S. All $-rentals must be converted at the rate of exchange of K25.02 Crowns = $1 and stored on the blocked account of IBM in Prague."

Schneider added that he met Watson's emissary, attorney Harrison K. Chauncey in Berlin, after the U.S. entered the war, to obtain IBM NY's permission to disguise German machines as Czech. "I made in 1942," Schneider reminded Watson, "with Mr. Chauncey, visiting Berlin, an agreement and so we were authorized to buy machines from the Dehomag and to sell or lend [lease] in our name. From each machine we had to pay a license-tax [royalty] to the IBM."

Watson was more than just a businessman selling boxes to the Third Reich. For his Promethean gift of punch card technology that enabled the Reich to achieve undreamed of efficiencies both in its rearmament program and its war against the Jews, for his refusal to join the chorus of strident anti-Nazi boycotters and isolators and instead open a commercial corridor the Reich could still navigate, for his willingness to bring the world's commercial summit to Berlin, for his glitter and legend, Hitler bestowed upon Watson a medal—the highest it could confer on any non-German.

The Merit Cross of the German Eagle with Star was created for Thomas Watson to "honor foreign nationals who made themselves deserving of the German Reich." It ranked second in prestige only to Hitler's German Grand Cross. Ultimately, several American corporate executives received this honor, including Henry Ford and GM's James Mooney. But Watson received it first.

In 1937, to receive his medal, Watson travelled to Berlin where he was honored at a festive Nazi banquet and extravaganza the likes of which the Reich had never seen. With Paul Goebbels as stage manager, the grateful Nazis would turn the event into a national homage to Thomas Watson and IBM. At the event, Watson was decorated with the swastika-bedecked sash and medal by *der Führer* himself. The IBM president kept the medal even after World War II broke out, even after the rape of Poland was fully underway. He did not return the prize until 1940 when France was bombed. But Watson maintained commercial relations with the Reich until the last moment.

Indeed, the last monthly rent check was given by a Reich representative to a U.S. Army officer in occupied Berlin in 1945. He told the Army man, "Please give this check to Mr. Watson."

Why did IBM do this? It was never about the anti-Semitism. It was never about the National Socialism. It was always about the money.

IBM's victim, Edjya, whose data was organized by IBM, survived her jump from the train speeding toward Treblinka. Her parents died. But she survived, hiding in the forest where she met her husband, Herschel. For two years Edjya and Herschel fought the Nazis as *partisans*, as forest fighters. After the war, they came to America. They changed their name to Black. They had a son. He devoted a decade of research and wrote this book precisely to determine what happened to the Jews of the Holocaust and what exactly was the pivotal Nazi Nexus.

———————

Sources: Primary documentation for this chapter is drawn exclusively from *IBM and the Holocaust* by Edwin Black.